hotels • restaurants • shops • spas

shanghaichic

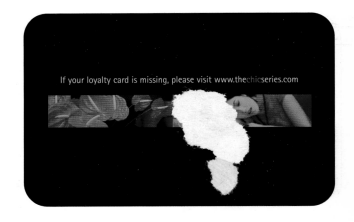

If your loyalty card is missing, please visit www.thechicseries.com

hotels • restaurants • shops • spas

shanghaichic

text barbara koh • zoë jaques

ARCHIPELAGO PRESS

THIS PAGE: Traditional rooftops at Yuyuan.

executive editor
melisa teo

senior editor
joanna greenfield

editor
lavinia ng

designers
annie teo • felicia wong

production manager
sin kam cheong

sales and marketing director
antoine monod

editions didier millet pte ltd
121 telok ayer street, #03-01
singapore 068590
email: edm@edmbooks.com.sg
website: www.edmbooks.com

first published 2006 • reprinted 2007
©2006 editions didier millet pte ltd

Printed in Singapore.

isbn: 981-4155-58-6
isbn-13: 978-981-4155-58-8

1		3		5		6		11		13		14			19
					4				12					20	
	2				7								17		
		8	9		10		15	16			18		21		

COVER CAPTIONS:

1: *Bold design at Shanghai Tang.*
2: *Detail at Longhua Temple.*
3: *Banyan Tree Spa Shanghai.*
4: *Sculpture at Face.*
5: *The bright lights of Nanjing Road.*
6: *One of Shanghai's grand villas.*
7: *Floral details at Fuchun Resort.*
8: *The canals of Suzhou.*
9: *Shanghai's popular snack xiao long bao.*
10: *Streets of Xintiandi.*
11: *Narrow alleys of the Old City.*
12: *The bird market of Shanghai.*
13: *Fish, symbols of prosperity and good luck.*
14: *Jin Mao Tower home to the Grand Hyatt.*
15: *Stylish detail at 88 Xintiandi.*
16: *Contemporary Chinese style.*
17: *Modern Shanghai.*
18: *Breakfast by the lake at Fuchun Resort.*
19: *Private dining room at Sens + Bund.*
20: *Shanghainese cuisine at Yè Shanghai.*
21: *Wan Hao Cantonese restaurant.*

PAGE 2: *The pinnacle of Jin Mao Tower.*

THIS PAGE: *Traditional rooftops at Yuyuan.*

OPPOSITE: *Space-age Pudong at night.*

PAGE 6: *The serenity of Hangzhou's West Lake.*

PAGE 8 AND 9: *Tai chi on the Bund.*

contents

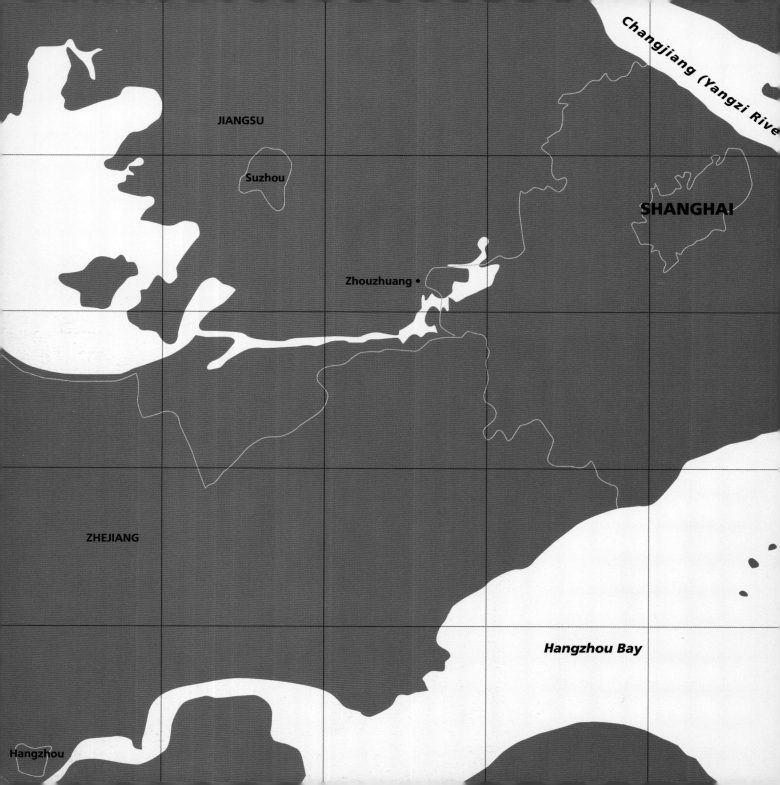

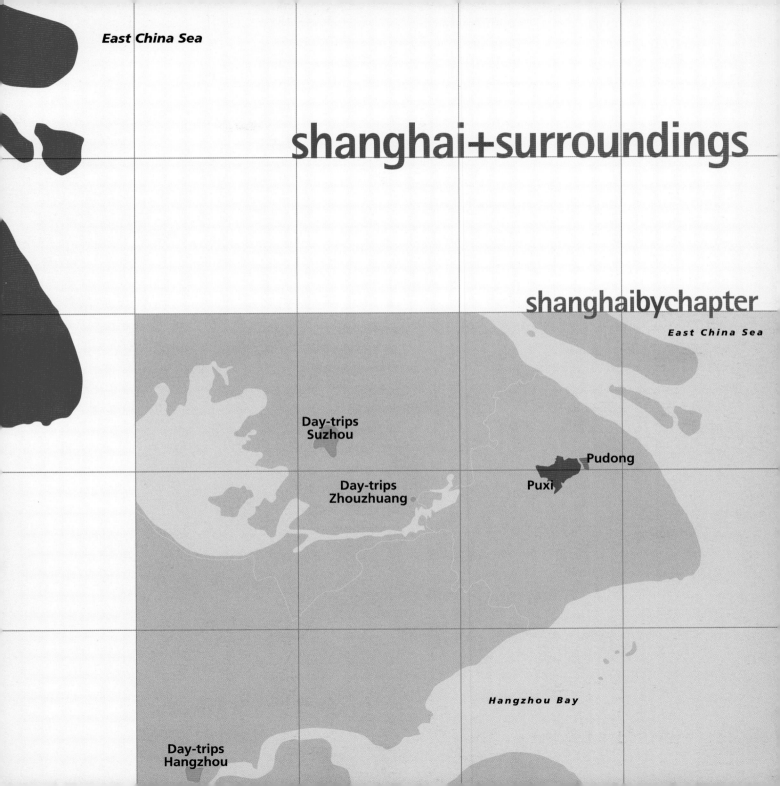

East China Sea

shanghai+surroundings

shanghaibychapter

East China Sea

**Day-trips
Suzhou**

**Day-trips
Zhouzhuang**

Pudong

Puxi

Hangzhou Bay

**Day-trips
Hangzhou**

introduction

A German-built train hurtles past a man in plastic sandals who's lugging a two-wheeled wooden cart laden with cardboard to recycle. A forest of glass and steel, including the highest hotel in the world and a spaceship-shaped pinnacle, faces neoclassical and Art Deco stone and brick edifices. Tycoons toast with a glass of Dom Perignon just around the corner from the first meeting site of the Chinese Communist Party. Shanghainese, Spanish and Japanese socialites shop for $1,000 party outfits a few blocks from where other Shanghainese women are emptying out chamber pots.

This is Shanghai. China and the West, materialist capitalism and Maoist Communism, the fabulously rich and miserably poor, cultures from every corner of the globe, and the past, present and future jostle together in this densest of Chinese cities. The chaotic mix is exhilarating, almost overwhelming, but not novel; Shanghai has long been the most cosmopolitan place in China, the most open to everyone and everything.

For nearly a century most of Shanghai was sectioned into enclaves self-governed by foreign nations. The booming trading port attracted entrepreneurs and later on, European refugees fleeing the Bolshevik Revolution and the Nazis, who brought their literature, arts, business know-how, architecture, urban planning, cuisine and socio-political theories with them. At the same time, intermittent anti-government rebellions and civil war drove Chinese from other provinces to the comparative safety of Shanghai. The city became mythic—for its wealth, modernity, high culture, vice, entertainment, fashion, intellectualism, debauchery and slums—and was dubbed the 'Paris of the East' as well as the 'Whore of the Orient'.

That life screeched to a halt once the Communists took over in 1949. But, allowed to get back on its feet in the early 1990s, Shanghai has since sprinted toward the future, with hardly a look back. Dominating the 21st century is China, and leading China is Shanghai. However, as dazzling as the frenetic push toward the future is, much of the city's character and chic-ness still emanates from the vestiges of its past. The real Shanghai is in its omnipresent juxtapositions and contrasts. That's what makes Shanghai today an endless fascination.

THIS PAGE: *A centuries-old picturesque and quiet water-canal town just outside Shanghai.*
OPPOSITE: *The Nanpu suspension bridge, one of the longest in the world, spans the Huangpu River.*

the city above the sea

Centuries ago, the place we know as Shanghai was wild marshland. Its first name was Hu Du (Hu Creek), derived from the hu, a bamboo fishing implement used by its inhabitants. But with its propitious location at the confluence of the Shanghai (which has long since disappeared) and the Huangpu rivers, the simple fishing community evolved into a port. During the Song Dynasty (960–1279), Shanghai continued to expand with the arrival of new immigrants escaping Mongol raiders in the north, the dredging of the swampy waterways and the building of canals. In 1074, government authorities upgraded the fishing village to the status of a 'commercial town'. In 1292, it was pronounced a county seat and officially named Shanghai, which means 'above the sea'. Shanghai was well on its way to more progress.

With the development of the textile industry during the Ming Dynasty (1368–1644), much of the region around Shanghai began cultivating cotton and weaving cloth. Later, the economy turned to growing indigo to produce blue fabric. Work continued on engineering and managing a network of navigable waters to access the country's interior. Shanghai blossomed into a major hub for ocean-going and river transportation and the trading of silk and tea. By 1553, the port had become prosperous enough to be the target of Japanese pirates, and the city's merchants funded the construction of a protective wall (around the present Old City) to deter them. A customs house was built in 1685. By the start of the 18th century, Shanghai's population had grown to 50,000.

the influx of opium

The British East India Company was one of the largest European traders with China, swapping silver, wool and spices for Chinese tea, silk and porcelain. However, the Qing Dynasty (1644–1911) government restricted foreign traders to only one port, Canton (now Guangzhou) in southern China. The British appetite for Chinese goods proved to be far greater than China's demand for Britain's offerings. In an attempt to even out the trade deficit, the British starting bringing opium, which had been grown and processed in India. Soon China was hooked. Too late, the Qing emperor declared a ban on opium imports. While imperial officials publicly accused Britain of pushing opium onto the Chinese, they themselves commonly smoked the drug and accepted kickbacks from British merchants. Opium was the single largest import into China (constituting more than 40 per cent of the country's total imports) in 1870. An estimated 10 per cent of the population smoked opium as of the late 1800s.

In 1839 the emperor's opium commissioner seized and destroyed some 1,350 tonnes of opium from British traders in Canton. Britain demanded compensation and access to more Chinese coastal ports; when the Qing government refused, Britain began assaults on various ports. In 1842, British navy ships sailed into the Yangzi and the Huangpu, and British soldiers swooped over the city walls and held Shanghai hostage. Defeated in the 1842 Opium War, the Chinese empire signed a treaty that opened five port cities (Shanghai, Ningbo, Fuzhou, Xiamen and Canton) to foreign commerce and allowed foreign nationals and consulates to take up residence in them.

foreign extraterritoriality

The US and France readily followed Britain's lead, forcing the weak empire to extend to them the same rights and benefits that Britain had won. Each of the three Western powers took over large chunks of Shanghai and turned them into separate, self-governed enclaves. (The British and American concessions later merged and became

THIS PAGE (FROM TOP): Neoclassical buildings on the Bund date back to the 1920s; Hongkou was a mostly Jewish and Chinese area in the 1930s and 1940s.

OPPOSITE (FROM LEFT): Suzhou Creek, lined with old warehouses; aside from opium, Shanghai was a trading hub for tea.

known as the International Settlement.) Immune from Chinese law and sovereignty, each settlement had its own police force, schools, courts, building code, sanitation and electric power system. During this time, Europeans, Americans, Japanese and Chinese alike flocked to Shanghai to start up businesses and try to make their fortunes. The city bustled with construction and commerce (including a still-active opium business). British trading houses that had prospered from opium revenues began dabbling in banking, real estate, infrastructure and insurance. Its strategic position in the middle of China's eastern seaboard and at the head of the Yangzi River, combined with the urban-planning expertise of its Western occupants, would prove a winning formula for turning Shanghai into the most advanced of China's cities, a distinction that has endured.

shanghai as sanctuary

Grumbling about corrupt Qing rule and profiteering Westerners gradually escalated into active revolt among the Chinese masses. The Taiping Rebellion (1850–64), which aimed to overthrow the Qing Dynasty, spread across the country. It also boosted Shanghai's population, as refugees poured into the city to escape the fighting in nearby regions. Rebels in fact attacked and seized Shanghai's Chinese walled section in 1853, before being quashed by Chinese imperial and French troops. The following year, Shanghai's foreign concessions organized the Shanghai Volunteer Corps, a militia to protect themselves. As hundreds of thousands of refugees continued to seek safety in Shanghai, the foreign settlements sold and leased land back to the local Chinese. Huge housing blocks mushroomed in the foreign enclaves, turning many real estate developers into fabulously rich tycoons.

Besides losing its grip at home, the Qing Dynasty lost many of its holdings in Korea and other parts of Asia to aggressive Western nations. In 1911, the Qing—China's last imperial dynasty—crumbled, and Sun Yatsen established the Republic of China and the Kuomintang (KMT), or Nationalist Party. Shanghai's ancient city walls were torn down. The new republic, however, was soon undermined by powerful warlords.

a city of extremes

The 20th century got underway with Shanghai leading the country in wealth, business, industry, finance, the arts and culture. It had acquired modern conveniences and trappings before the rest of China, such as electricity, motorcars, electric trams and cinemas. It had the tallest buildings, the most banks and automobiles and the chicest fashion. Foreign capitalists who'd made their millions in Shanghai and Chinese mob bosses built mansions, private clubs and racetracks. In the far eastern parts of the city, Britons would re-enact their beloved fox hunts, with horses and hounds trampling farmers' fields. The effervescent nightlife options ranged from highbrow concerts to seedy brothels. As the only city in the world that did not require passports, Shanghai was wide open, not only to Chinese but also to foreign refugees and migrants. They were resourceful, resilient and entrepreneurial, with often shady pasts. Shanghai earned several nicknames during this time, among them, the 'Paradise for Adventurers', 'Paris of the East' and 'Whore of the Orient'. By the mid-1930s, it was home to about 70,000 Japanese, White Russians, Jews and other non-Chinese, who formed their own social groups including the Boy Scouts, Det Norske and the Iranian, Missouri, and Shanghai Homing Pigeon clubs.

However, even in their 1930s heyday, foreigners amounted to a mere sliver of Shanghai's 3.5 million residents (in terms of population, Shanghai was the world's fifth-largest city). For the majority, life was nasty, brutish, impoverished and short. Over-worked and exploited in mostly foreign-owned textile factories and crammed into dingy tenement blocks, Shanghai's Chinese lived to an average age of just 27 years old, equivalent to the life expectancy of Europeans during the Middle Ages. According to an official count, in 1937, 20,000 homeless people died in the city that year.

rumblings of communism

Given the rising income inequality, the city's intellectuals, students and workers became receptive to new and radical political theories. The first meeting of the Chinese Communist Party was held in Shanghai, in 1921. In May 1925, a Japanese

THIS PAGE (FROM TOP): *The former French Concession evokes a true feel for 'Paris of the East', and is pleasant for an afternoon walk; wander down side streets for glimpses of everyday life.*
OPPOSITE: *Xintiandi's revamped shikumen were once homes to thousands of Shanghainese.*

textile-mill supervisor in Shanghai shot and killed a Chinese labourer, which sparked street demonstrations against foreign domination. British police opened fire on 30 May, killing more Chinese. In the ensuing 30 May Movement, strikes erupted in Shanghai and quickly spread to other Chinese cities.

In 1927, Kuomintang leader Chiang Kaishek announced that in alliance with the Chinese Communist Party, he wanted to remove the country's various warlords and imperialists from power and unite China. Embarking on what became known as the Northern Expedition, Chiang then led his KMT army northward from its base in Guangzhou. Chiang's true intentions, though, were not so pure. After reaching Shanghai, KMT soldiers, with the assistance of manpower, guns, and money from mafia leader Du Yuesheng, rounded up and gunned down thousands of Communists and labour organizers. The White Terror massacre in Shanghai was just one of Chiang Kaishek's campaigns over the next few years to snuff out Chinese Communists. As a result civil war erupted.

THIS PAGE: Barges ply the Huangpu just as they did centuries ago.

OPPOSITE: About 20,000 Jewish refugees from Europe made northern Shanghai their home during World War II.

the japanese era

In 1931, Japan invaded and took over Manchuria, the first step of its scheme to claim all of China. Shanghainese began a boycott of Japanese products. Arguments and fights broke out between Chinese and Japanese, which Japan then used as a rationale to air-bomb and demolish a poor Chinese district of Shanghai. Chinese refugees fled to the International Settlement for safety.

By 1937, it was all-out war between Japan and China. Chiang Kaishek, who had set up his headquarters in Chongqing, committed his best soldiers to defend Shanghai, but they were defeated in a well-coordinated Japanese attack in August. Japan then ruled the city except for the French and International concessions, which remained under the governance of Westerners. Many expatriates, though, began leaving Shanghai for safer havens.

After its December 1941 bombing raid on the United States' Pearl Harbor, Japan took control of the foreign enclaves in Shanghai. The Japanese interrogated and tortured suspicious Allied nationals, and later corralled the rest into prison camps. In 1943 the Allied countries agreed to relinquish to the KMT their rights over Shanghai's foreign settlements—even though the territories were under Japan's thumb. The power and privileges that Westerners had enjoyed throughout Shanghai for nearly a century came to an abrupt end.

Japan's occupation drained Shanghai. Elderly Shanghainese today can still recall how Japanese patrols stopped and harassed ordinary Chinese on the streets. Inflation soared and factories were made to work overtime to support Japan's war effort.

continued civil war

After Japan surrendered in 1945, the KMT took back control of Shanghai and turned to its battle against China's Communists. The Communist Party, however, had built up its support significantly during the anti-Japanese war years and had managed to expand its stronghold in northern China. Leaving its northern base, the People's

Liberation Army headed south. In May 1949, it marched into and 'liberated' Shanghai. By autumn that year, the People's Liberation Army had taken control of all of the key cities along the coast and in the south. On 1 October 1949 in Beijing—Communist leader—Mao Zedong announced the birth of the People's Republic of China. "The Chinese people have stood up," he declared. Chiang Kaishek escaped to Taiwan, where he named Taipei as the capital of the Republic of China.

the new people's republic

After 1949, China turned inward, and closed itself off from much of the rest of the world. The newly empowered Chinese Communist Party proceeded to take over private businesses and property and to clean up Shanghai. Brothels and opium dens were closed, child labour was banned, and prostitutes and drug addicts were given 're-education'. Foreign companies and nationals evacuated Shanghai. Many of the city's successful, most talented and most educated Chinese, including accountants, doctors, shipping executives, artists and tailors, slipped away to Hong Kong and Taiwan (if they hadn't already).

The Communist Party's modus operandi was to orchestrate campaigns and programmes with assorted objectives, such as to stamp out corruption or drug use, promote gender equality, rail against American imperialism, halt bourgeoisie frivolities, and most importantly silence critics, from either the left or the right. All of Shanghai's dance halls were closed by 1954. The population donned unisex jackets and trousers in drab blue or grey. Shanghai was fortunate to be largely spared one of the most disastrous movements, the Great Leap Forward (1958–61). Mao's goal was to catch up with the West's level of industrialization, through collectivization and mass labour; peasants were instructed to produce steel using backyard steel furnaces. Instead, the Leap caused the worst famine in world history, in which about 30 million Chinese people died. (By comparison, Stalin killed approximately 10 million of his subjects either through execution or starvation.)

THIS PAGE: **Portraits of Mao are becoming a rare sight in modern Shanghai.**

OPPOSITE (FROM LEFT): **A Little Red Book of Mao's sayings; a statue of Chen Yi, Shanghai's first Communist mayor, presides over the throngs and traffic at the Bund, against the backdrop of the Oriental Pearl TV Tower that stands across the river.**

The Communist Party kept extremely tight reins on all parts of society by organizing administrative units at each workplace and in each neighbourhood. The units, that were headed by Party loyalists, assigned individuals to jobs (often having little or no relation to one's skills or interests), announced and enforced Beijing's latest edicts and closely monitored people's daily lives. Indeed, in order to wed, a prospective bride and groom were even required to first obtain the approval of their work units.

cultural revolution

In 1966, Mao Zedong unleashed the Cultural Revolution, purportedly to re-ignite China's revolutionary spirit, but essentially to attack his perceived political enemies. He made Shanghai the epicentre of the new Revolution. There, the Gang of Four, which included his wife, took on much of the direction and choreography of the movement. (Jiang Qing, Mao's wife and a former B-movie actress, took advantage of her power to persecute Shanghai Film Studio colleagues who'd slighted her years earlier.)

For the next decade, youths and workers were exhorted to transform into Red Guards, zealots who recited like automatons from the Little Red Book of Mao's sayings. Their raison d'être, they were instructed, was to eradicate the 'four olds' in China, old customs, old habits, old culture and old thinking. Raiding homes, they burned Western and Chinese classical books and paintings and smashed family heirlooms and Chinese antiques. Students ridiculed, spat on and beat their teachers—and anyone else with an intellectual, capitalist or bourgeois background, even their parents. Formal education was suspended. Entertainment was restricted to a short list of revolutionary operas and ballets approved by Jiang Qing. Factions of Red Guards competed to demonstrate which was the most ardently 'red'. In Shanghai, St. Ignatius Cathedral's two towers were chopped off and the Jing'An Temple was damaged. Many buildings in the former foreign concessions were ransacked, and the Bund was renamed 'Revolution Boulevard'. During the Cultural Revolution, one million Shanghainese were sent to the countryside—they were to learn about revolution by toiling alongside the peasantry.

capitalist awakening

After Mao died in 1976, the Gang of Four were imprisoned, tried and blamed for most of the killings and other crimes of the Revolution. Deng Xiaoping became the country's supreme leader in 1978, and quickly introduced pragmatic, economic reforms and a policy of 'opening up' China to the rest of the world. Since then, the Chinese government has continued steering the country in a capitalist direction. China's economy has become one of the fastest growing in the world.

Although the ruling Chinese Communist Party has been relatively generous with economic reform, political reform is considered an entirely different beast. Official corruption and rising inflation led to massive pro-democracy demonstrations in Beijing's Tiananmen Square in the spring of 1989. The peaceful protest, which on some days attracted 0.5–1 million supportive citizens to the streets, was led by students. The

THIS PAGE: Tiananmen Square in Beijing, where Mao announced the birth of the People's Republic in 1949 and short-lived pro-democracy demonstrations were held 40 years later.

OPPOSITE (FROM TOP): Cultural Revolution heroes for sale at a Dongtai Road antiques stall; a red army soldier.

Communist hard-liners in the leadership demanded that order be restored. After almost two months, on June 4, the democracy movement ended when the People's Liberation Army was sent to clear out the crowds in and around the square.

Students in Shanghai also demonstrated in the streets that spring. But in response, Shanghai mayor Zhu Rongji directed thousands of workers from state-owned companies to go and talk with and calm the protestors. His strategy worked. The students disbanded and returned to their campuses; Zhu kept the peace without having to use martial law or force. Jiang Zemin, the city's Communist Party Secretary and a former mayor, shut down a local newspaper that had supported the demonstrators.

Deng Xiaoping took notice. Soon after the Tiananmen protests, Deng designated Jiang as his successor. Jiang Zemin became president in 1993. In 1998, Zhu Rongji, who also won acclaim for the development of Pudong and the rapid modernization of Shanghai's infrastructure, was named China's premier. A charismatic straight talker, Zhu launched economic reforms and anti-corruption campaigns, managed to steer the country through Asia's financial crisis of the late 1990s and secured China's entry to the World Trade Organization.

from strength to strength

With the ascendancy of Jiang Zemin and Zhu Rongji, China is on the road to socialist modernization. In 2003, Hu Jintao, who had been identified by Deng Xiaoping as a future leader, succeeded Jiang Zemin as president. Zhu Rongji was replaced by a protégé of his, Wen Jiabao. Like their predecessors, both president Hu and premier Wen are trained engineers, but they have stronger ties to China's interior (rather than the relatively properous and urbane coast).

After taking over the reins of leadership, Hu and his premier Wen have given more attention to build a 'harmonious society', advocating growth stability, broader welfare benefits and state support for social security.

THIS PAGE (FROM TOP): Nanjing Road, Shanghai's popular shopping street, signals the mass consumerism of new Shanghai; while the hammer and sickle signify the union of industrial and agricultural labour in a Communist system.
OPPOSITE: High-fashion mural advertising.

...steering the country in a capitalist direction.

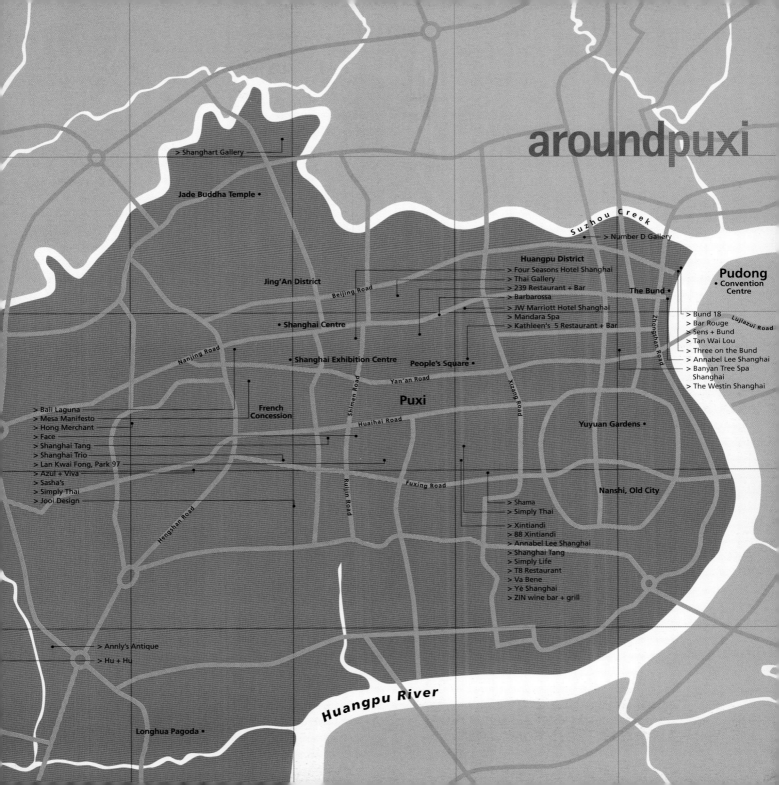

aroundpuxi

Suzhou Creek

> Number D Gallery

> Shanghart Gallery

Jade Buddha Temple •

Huangpu District
> Four Seasons Hotel Shanghai
> Thai Gallery
> 239 Restaurant + Bar
> Barbarossa
> JW Marriott Hotel Shanghai
> Mandara Spa
> Kathleen's 5 Restaurant + Bar

Jing'An District

Beijing Road

The Bund •

Pudong
• Convention Centre

> Bund 18
> Bar Rouge
> Sens + Bund
> Tan Wai Lou
> Three on the Bund
> Annabel Lee Shanghai
> Banyan Tree Spa Shanghai
> The Westin Shanghai

Lujiazui Road

Shanghai Centre •

Nanjing Road

Shanghai Exhibition Centre •

Yan'an Road

People's Square •

Zhongshan Road

Puxi

Shimen Road

Xizang Road

French Concession

Yuyuan Gardens •

Huaihai Road

> Bali Laguna
> Mesa Manifesto
> Hong Merchant
> Face
> Shanghai Tang
> Shanghai Trio
> Lan Kwai Fong, Park 97
> Azul + Viva
> Sasha's
> Simply Thai
> Jooi Design

Ruijin Road

Fuxing Road

Nanshi, Old City

Hengshan Road

> Shama
> Simply Thai

> Xintiandi
> 88 Xintiandi
> Annabel Lee Shanghai
> Shanghai Tang
> Simply Life
> T8 Restaurant
> Va Bene
> Yè Shanghai
> ZIN wine bar + grill

> Annly's Antique
> Hu + Hu

Huangpu River

Longhua Pagoda •

a unique persona

Sophisticated, image-conscious, worldly and proud, the Shanghainese are the New Yorkers of China. They have ambition in spades, which, combined with their street-smarts, versatility and networks of family and friends, has been the springboard to riches and renown. They're China's wealthiest citizens. They are the first in the country to sport coiffures and fashions fresh from the catwalks of Paris, New York, Milan and Tokyo. They're the first to be able to lip-synch the lyrics to Asia's top hits, whether they're Taiwan blues or Japanese rap, and the first to spread the latest gossip about Nicole Kidman, Bill Gates, Zhang Ziyi and Jackie Chan. Louis Vuitton, Boucheron, Jean Paul Gaultier, Tiffany, Cartier and other exclusive brands have tended to set up shop in Shanghai before venturing anywhere else in China. Meanwhile, Chinese in other areas of the country may call the Shanghainese haughty and shallow, but they look on with envy and admiration.

international company

From its early days, Shanghai has been a magnet for immigrants and refugees of all types—individuals of assorted economic levels, ethnicities and nationalities. It flourished as a port and as the hub of a regional textile industry. Its commercial significance surged even higher after the Chinese imperial government lost the Opium Wars in the early 1840s and was forced to open Shanghai and other treaty ports to international trade and settlement.

Chinese from the south and the interior of the country migrated to Shanghai and took up jobs as manual labourers, compradors, bookkeepers and shopkeepers. Europeans, Americans and Japanese invested and built bank headquarters, private membership clubs, factories, insurance co mpanies and apartments. Chinese fleeing the cross-fire between the ruling government and insurgents, Russians running from the Bolsheviks, Jews seeking haven from the Nazis, people escaping persecution, secrets or past lives: over time, they all ended up in Shanghai.

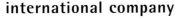

PAGE 26: Longhua Temple, Shanghai's largest temple.

THIS PAGE: Some of the city's trend-setters enjoying the impressive opening party for Armani, just one of the designer brands enjoying local demand.

OPPOSITE: Shanghai's popular Nanjing Road, home to shopping galore.

They are the foundation of the city's pre-eminence. A former mayor was once asked about the popular belief that the smartest people in China are from Shanghai. His response: "The smartest are not from Shanghai—they come to Shanghai." Today, this inflow continues.

character building

Tough circumstances build character, as the saying goes. In Shanghai, the character that has developed is reputed to be driven by money—as well as skilled at making it. Such a knack for business, along with the clever and calculating Shanghainese mind, means one must be on the ball when dealing with them, other Chinese say. But although the locals are said to be guarded, they are also capable, efficient and ultra-pragmatic. They are willing to stretch and compromise; foreign executives attest that overall it's easier to get things accomplished here than elsewhere in China.

Shanghainese are also competitive and conspicuous consumers. Comparing pedigree and status—on criteria such as schooling, occupation, employer and income—and keeping up with the Lis are common practices. Sales and service sectors in the city have been riddled with high turnover lately, since many young professionals will jump from one employer to the next for pay increases or more impressive job titles. One quirky piece of conventional wisdom says that the higher priced an item is (whether it is cheesecake, a suit or hospital care), the better quality it must be.

Because Shanghainese put a high priority on image, they typically are ardent fans of luxury labels. For those who can't afford or don't want to buy the real thing, the markets are bursting with Prada, Hermes, Chanel and DKNY knock-offs. Those with hefty wallets like to continuously upgrade their cell phones, iPods, and cars and be seen at the newest and swankiest clubs. Most locals live on far less, yet they still pay attention to their outward appearance. In public Shanghainese look well-groomed and walk with dignity, which shows an innate sense of style, some Western fashion designers say; a slovenly or unkempt Shanghainese is a rare sight.

outside influences

The Shanghai persona is also inclined to be flexible and accepting, even welcoming, of outside influences, perhaps a legacy of the city's history. Proud of their hometown, the Shanghainese are anxious about how it stacks up against international standards. Locals gobble up pop culture from abroad and don't have the blind nationalism that some of their compatriots have. The employers of choice are foreign corporations, the chicest restaurants in town are French and Japanese, and the universal hope is to travel abroad. Shanghai-natives (especially the women) frequently date and occasionally marry expatriates. Multinationals say Shanghai's is the most progressive of the local

THIS PAGE: The Giorgio Armani store at Three on the Bund entices brand-loving window shoppers as they pass by.

OPPOSITE (FROM TOP): An enterprising Shanghainese; foreign franchises have become commonplace in Shanghai.

Chinese governments in terms of adhering to WTO requirements.

Open-mindedness has limits even in Shanghai, however. Often locals can be quick to label and denigrate other Chinese as wai di, from the outside, implying that they're too boorish, uneducated or dishevelled to be Shanghainese. Yet at the same time, the Shanghainese realize that they depend on these outsiders to enhance their own lives—to build their homes, clean, drive, babysit, collect trash and do other menial work.

a language all of its own

Mandarin is the official language of China. As written, it is a uniform set of characters that evolved from ancient pictographs. As spoken—well, that's when any semblance of uniformity collapses. China's complicated geography and history resulted in a national landscape that is dotted with innumerable and motley dialects. Provinces and even towns have their own dialects, which are difficult—if not impossible—for non-locals to decipher. The purest and most accurate forms of Mandarin are spoken by the Chinese in Beijing and further north.

Shanghai has its own tongue, which sounds wholly foreign to non-Shanghainese. When it's time to bid goodbye, for instance, instead of saying the Mandarin 'zai jian', Shanghainese toss out 'ze wei'. There are campaigns to promote the use of Mandarin, but Shanghainese much prefer to chatter in their own dialect. They have their pick of Shanghai-dialect news, sitcoms, radio shows and plays.

Like French, the Shanghainese dialect is fluid and soft. It sounds especially melodic and pretty when spoken by women. This gentle tone can be somewhat misleading, as Shanghainese women are frequently mentioned as forceful and iron-willed, veiled

THIS PAGE: *New Heights Bar, one of Shanghai's many watering holes.*

OPPOSITE (FROM TOP): *The women in Shanghai keep abreast of the latest fashion trends found in popular magazines; exercising with a view.*

behind a kitten-like façade. Shanghai men, who are said to be family-centric and good househusband material, often accompany women on shopping excursions to carry their handbags and purchases.

enduring concepts and habits

Despite Shanghai's yearning to fast-forward to the future, it clings onto several traditional Chinese beliefs and behaviours. Some are so deeply rooted that they seem almost genetic. Even if your visit to Shanghai is ultra-short, you're likely to witness at least one of them.

Guanxi—meaning connections—greases the wheels. Whether it's obtaining bureaucrats' approval to build a golf course, securing a Saturday night reservation at a popular restaurant, or getting a cheaper price from an underwear peddler, if you have a connection to the powers-that-be (or at least a connection to a connection), problems seem to fade and things happen faster. Guanxi is especially critical in business circles. Marathon karaoke nights and ten-course banquets are frequently guanxi-building sessions in loose disguise.

Even in the midst of arguments and confrontation, Chinese generally try to preserve everyone's mianzi (face), dignity or self-pride. Losing face—being subjected to public embarrassment—is regarded as a grave insult, and a seemingly casual comment or joke could be taken utlra-seriously. For example, one loses face if he or she is forced to admit defeat or is the target of outright criticism (even if it is well-intentioned or true) or personal attacks. Thus, rather than voicing temper tantrums and direct rejections, Chinese are inclined to compromise. In the face of an impossible request, a Chinese person might side-step it and reply that fulfilling the request would be 'inconvenient'. Or he might consent or agree—keeping a smiling visage all the while—and then simply ignore it. In both instances, he preserves the face of the requester and himself.

Traditional Confucian values are strong amongst the people of Shanghai. Respect for the elderly and for scholars has survived vicious propaganda movements such as the Cultural Revolution, and the Shanghainese are still very family-oriented.

Three's not a crowd. A present dearth of affordable housing in the cities and a history since the 1950s of government-mandated collectives, communes, and other group-living arrangements and experiments have tended to squelch any fantasies of personal space. (Even Chinese tradition defines the ideal household as containing three generations under one roof.) In density, as in so many other categories, Shanghai is distinguished: it is the most crowded of all municipalities and provinces in the country. Queues, elevators, department stores and museums often become collections of humanity, squeezing and pushing. Many local restaurants accommodate lunch-hour crowds by nudging separate parties to share one table.

The Shanghai government is trying to bring some order to the subways. Regular announcements squawking through loudspeakers and Chinese characters painted on the platform instruct people that before piling in, they should allow passengers to step out. Once inside the train, however, passengers are likely to find ponytails, shopping bags, elbows or other body parts in their faces.

Public displays of personal hygiene habits are an enduring ritual amongst the Chinese. A low rumble, then a crescendo and finally, HHAAUCKK! Yet another spit-wad hits the sidewalk; yet another respiratory passageway is clear of phlegm. During the SARS epidemic in 2003, China's government enacted a fine and a furious media drive to stop spitting. The practice subsided. Once the health threat seemed to pass, many spitters revved up again. The fine for spitting in a public place is RMB200, but it is rarely levied. However, spitting is less commonplace in China now than pre-SARS. It's also less practised in Shanghai than in the rest of the country.

Regarding other typical, publicly displayed habits—such as smoking, littering, nose-picking—the Shanghai government hopes that its recent campaign touting civility and a civilized society will tidy up people's manners—and the pavement.

...Shanghainese look well-groomed and walk with dignity, which shows an innate sense of style...

This is a city that doesn't take food or mealtimes lightly.

food as an occasion

It's difficult to walk more than two blocks in Shanghai and not run into a source of food, and it is difficult to get bored with it. China's famously cosmopolitan metropolis is a culinary smorgasbord with the quantity and the variety to keep a foodie stuffed with local and not-so-local delights. There's food from every region in the country, plus foreign cuisines such as Turkish, Vietnamese, Japanese and German.

One can choose meatloaf and a swivelling red stool in an American '50s-style diner with jukebox rock 'n roll, or a hotter-than-hell Hunan dinner with plenty of Tsingdao and flush-faced businessmen. Croissants and borscht, introduced by the French and the White Russians during the foreign-concession years, are still popular. Savour foie gras seared, moussed, baked, sautéed, and stuffed in ravioli; get your truffle fix with truffle pizza followed by truffle ice cream. International chains are here in force, including Starbucks, Delifrance, Manabe Coffee, Papa John's Pizza, Hippopotamus, Hooters, and of course McDonalds.

This is a city that doesn't take food or mealtimes lightly. Meals are not just for eating; rather, they're occasions to schmooze, reunite and reciprocate. In image-fixated Shanghai, hosting a banquet of delicacies is an opportunity to boost one's status and build face. Hence, a lot of time is spent around food.

an international twist

Beginning with the whirlwind 1990s, the dining scene has gone upscale as people have become richer and more private entrepreneurs have ventured into restaurants. Dining in Shanghai is fancier and pricier each year. Michelin-star chefs from Europe serve the filet mignon with braised oxtail and the lobster terrine that earned them the stars back home, and without reservations, you might be turned away on the Bund, even on weeknights. Chaine des Rotisseurs' invitation-only dinners are a hot item. Old concession-era villas and historic landmarks are transformed into plush eateries that play up the architecture and nostalgia.

THIS PAGE: *A blend of Western and Asian food, tapas style from 239, is just one example of Shanghai's culinary fusions.*

OPPOSITE: *Sumptuous dining at Laris, one of Three on the Bund's fine dining restaurants with stunning views of the Bund.*

In 2004, Zagat Survey published its first restaurant guide to Shanghai—the first in Asia other than Japan. The shift upmarket is making its biggest waves in Chinese cuisine, with chic, pricey Chinese restaurants rushing onstage and stagnant state-run eateries on the out. Chefs who have been overseas and back are whipping up 'reinterpretations' of traditional Chinese dishes that are spiked with foreign accents, making the food all the more interesting.

the land of fish and rice

Shanghai is a paradise of Chinese food, particularly its own. Although not as widely known overseas as Cantonese cuisine, Shanghainese fare holds more substance and interest for many foodies. Shanghai is fortunate to be sitting in 'the land of fish and rice', a region so dubbed because of its fertile ground and major rivers teeming with fresh catch.

THIS PAGE: Xiao long bao makers, passers-by can stop and revel in the process of making these Shanghainese favourites.

OPPOSITE (FROM TOP): A noodle-maker shows off his skills; food stalls on street corners are a common sight.

With its countryside origins, the local cuisine is homey, stick-to-your-ribs stuff that's oilier and sweeter than other Chinese varieties. Its rich sauces make liberal use of ginger, rice wine of nearby Shaoxing, soy sauce and sugar. They're the kind of sauces that people can't resist sopping up to the last drop, with plain, hot rice. Food is usually stir-fried, 'red-cooked' (hong shao) in rock-sugar and soy sauce, braised in clay pots or 'drunken' (marinated in Shaoxing rice wine).

From the very beginning of a meal, Shanghainese cuisine shows its style and abundance. Hors d'oeuvres, meticulously laid out in geometric and flowery patterns, include pickled vegetables, drunken chicken, al dente edame, marinated mushrooms, lightly mashed beans and minced greens and dried pressed bean curd. Cooks use the best local produce of each season; in spring, for instance, Shanghai's house specials include pudgy bamboo shoots that are red-cooked.

On the heartier side, there are lion's head meatballs, ground pork pounded until velvety and shaped into rounds the size of softballs. One of the best-loved Shanghainese dishes is tipang, pork rump that is left to simmer for hours in a dark, rich sauce. By the time it reaches the table, the meat is so tender that applying a knife to it or even chewing seems excessive. And any remaining sauce begs to be soaked up with rice.

What's for dessert? Usually fresh fruit such as oranges or watermelon. There's also tang yuan, dumplings made of rice flour and commonly stuffed with sesame seeds, ground peanuts and sugar, or red bean paste. Eight-jewel rice, a sort of sweet, sticky-pudding version of the conventional fried rice, is studded with jewels such as maraschino cherries, lotus seeds, chopped candied fruit and walnuts.

Desserts for a more Western palate are even easier to find. Bakeries throughout Shanghai make airy sponge and chiffon layer cakes, blanketed in clouds of whipped icing and adorned with fruit.

Given Shanghai's geographical location, bounty from both ocean and river waters features prominently on the menu: stir-fried river eel, red-cooked yellow croaker, crystal prawns (marinated in egg whites and then lightly sautéed), and smoked cod are just a

few of the classics. The most famous and prized of all of Shanghai's water-foods is dazha crab, a creature only a few inches wide with black hairy legs. The Shanghai hairy crab's very hairy legs are not the prettiest sight, but the roe is exquisitely creamy (rapture-inducing, some connoisseurs say) and the meat is fragrant and succulent. Usually the crab is simply steamed.

Although the crab craze has spawned crab farms across the region, purists say the best crabs still come from the depths of Yangcheng Lake in neighbouring Jiangsu Province. Hairy crabs make an all-too-brief annual appearance in autumn, when gourmets across Asia scurry to Shanghai to indulge in the speciality.

snack-heaven

Between or after meals, you needn't go hungry. Shanghai is a city that snacks. Roving peddlers, little storefronts, and street stands all offer fast-food that's not necessarily junk food. In the wintertime, street vendors sell hot roasted chestnuts from carts and baked sweet potatoes from big metal drums. During the spring and summer months, they hawk melon slices, ice cream and caramelized strawberries on skewers.

Year-round, there are bao zi, steamed buns stuffed with sweet bean paste, vegetables or meat, luobo cibing, a flaky pastry with shredded turnip inside, and you tiao, a deep-fried, long dough twist that locals like for breakfast. Shengjian mantou is another favourite—pork-filled buns that are first steamed and then pan-fried.

If there's one food item that all Shanghainese crave, it's xiao long bao (literally little steamer-basket buns). Shanghai's answer to Hong Kong's dim sum was actually invented in the village of Nanxiang village, to the north of Shanghai. The delicate steamed dumplings consist of a pork mixture encased in thin wrappers of dough. They are brought to the table still in the steamer basket, and it takes some patience and agility to extract one, dip it in a mixture of soy sauce, vinegar and shredded ginger, and transfer it to your mouth intact. Once you do so, however, you'll know why xiao long bao are close to Shanghainese people's hearts and you may develop a craving for these buns yourself.

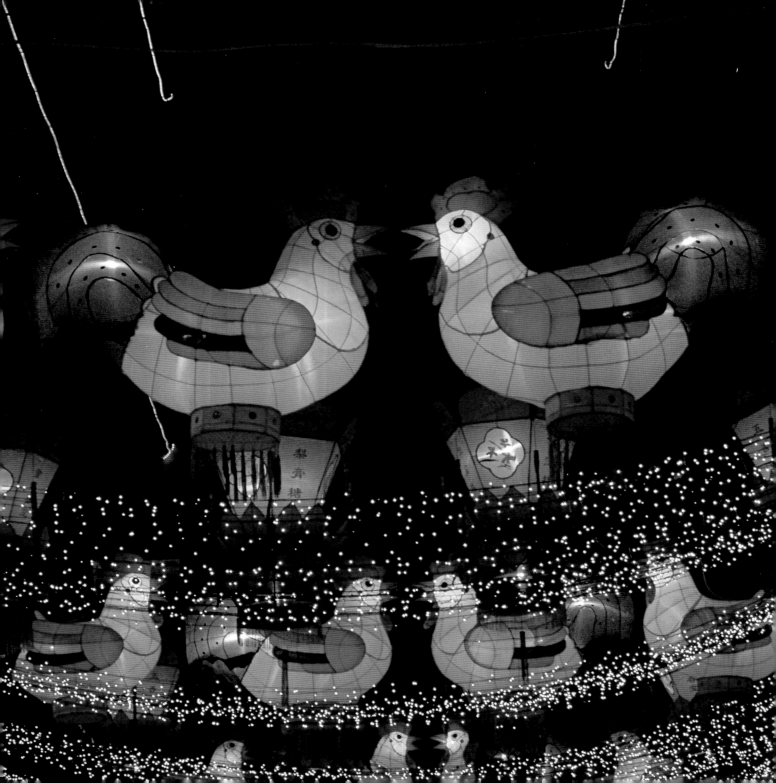

cultural calendar

Traditional Chinese culture, which follows a calendar based on the moon's phases, is adorned with festivals and holidays that pay homage to ancestors and gods. Chinese communities in Asia and the West observe them with time-honoured ceremonies, rituals and feasts, but under communism on the Chinese mainland, much of this vitality has faded. At the same time, young people in China are eagerly embracing modern Western culture and practices, including holidays. Increasing numbers of young Shanghainese are exchanging Christmas cards and gifts and even buying artificial fir trees to put in their living rooms. Restaurants mark 14 February with candlelit dinners of Champagne and oysters.

Spring Festival, or Chinese New Year—the mother of all Chinese festivals—is a two-week, joyful gala to usher in a new lunar year. It is a family-oriented celebration, in which children near and far return to their parents' nests. China's family reunion translates into 40 million people on the move every day—and has been described as the world's biggest annual migration. Public transportation systems are clogs of chaos stuffed and stretched beyond imagination. Lugging vinyl bags bulging with gifts, money and new clothes, migrant workers on trains cram into every speck and sliver of space inside and between the cars. Many have to stand for entire 36- or 72-hour journeys, enduring a monotony of clacking, rocking and sweaty smells.

By New Year's Eve, the house must be spick and span and all debts must be paid, so that one has a fresh start for the year. The family sits down to a sumptuous dinner of symbolic foods—a whole and intact fish to signify abundance, stringy seaweed whose name sounds like 'good fortune', and so on. In Shanghai a round-shaped pasta made of rice flour is also traditionally served. The chewy, slightly sticky nian gao (new-year cake) is an omen of family unity and harmony. Firecrackers, which started popping randomly during the day, let out a regular rat-tat-tat by nightfall. Crowds mill around the Bund, where the Shanghai government stages a fireworks extravaganza. From about 11 p.m. until the early hours of New Year's Day, the firecracker cacophony is

THIS PAGE (FROM TOP): Stores display their festive decorations; the colourful dragon dance is a must-have in every Chinese New Year celebration.
OPPOSITE: Lanterns adorn the streets during the festivities.

continuous and the sky is a blur of smoke. On New Year's Day, families circulate to the homes of relatives and friends, bearing fruit, cookies or candy. They hand out hongbao, small red envelopes with cash tucked inside, to children and singles.

Spring Festival usually falls in January or February. In recent years, China's government has extended the allotted vacation days, reasoning that if people have more time off, they'll shop and spend more, which will help the economy more. Thus, workers in China have been getting at least a week off for Spring Festival. In contrast, Taiwan, Hong Kong, Singapore and most other Asian countries schedule only two or three days off for the lunar New Year.

THIS PAGE: **Shop for local produce, trinkets, handicraft, tea and hawker food at Yuyuan Bazaar.**

OPPOSITE (FROM TOP): **Youngsters are treated to a good time on Children's Day; during the Dragon Boat Festival, teams row to the pace of drums.**

causes for celebration

Lantern Festival marks the first full moon of the lunar year; people stroll through the streets and parks, swinging colourful lanterns. Peddlers and shops carry a dazzling selection of lanterns—made of paper, fabric or hard plastic, in conventional, floral, animal and cartoon-character shapes, illuminated by tiny bulbs. The Lantern Festival, held on the 15th day of the 1st lunar month, is also regarded as the end of Spring Festival. Yuyuan Gardens sets up an exhibit of hand-crafted lanterns. Needless to say, this day is a fun-filled one, especially for the children.

Soon after is International Women's Day on 8 March. This day is set aside to pay tribute to China's women, who, the government says, 'hold up half the sky'.

In early April the Chinese hold the Qing Ming Festival—or 'Tomb-Sweeping Day'—to show respect to their ancestors. They trek to the gravesites of their family members to pull out encroaching weeds and clean up the sites, burn paper money (for the deceased to use in the afterlife), and leave bouquets of flowers and offerings of food.

May Day is celebrated in China and is ostensibly a holiday to honour the workers of the world. For most Chinese, however, it is significant because it means another week off from work. And unlike traditional Chinese festivals, it is not riddled with rituals, tasks and family obligations.

International Children's Day is held on 1 June. Youngsters are treated to toys, games, ice cream bars and less-arduous classes. Arguably, though, every day in China is Children's Day. In the 1970s, Beijing announced that a couple would be allowed to have only one child. The consensus—among both the masses and officials—is that the one-child policy has controlled population growth, as intended, but has also bred a generation of spoiled children.

The Dragon Boat Festival memorializes a righteous statesman of the 3rd century BC. Qu Yuan, a respected official and poet, drowned himself to protest the corruption in his government. Sympathetic citizens cooked dollops of meat, sweet beans and glutinous rice wrapped inside lotus leaves. They threw them into the river, in hopes that

the fish would nibble at the zongzi bundles rather than Qu's body. To mark the festival at Dianshan Lake, colourful elongated boats of crew teams race to the fast pace of the drums. The festival, on the 5th day of the 5th lunar month, falls in May or June.

On the 15th night of the 8th lunar month (usually in late September or early October), the moon is said to be at its fullest. The harvest has been completed and so the Moon Festival begins. Family members reunite over a feast and share moon cakes. The moon cake, the star of the festival, is a plump, round pastry—the shape of an ice-hockey puck—and is filled with mashed beans, lotus seeds, minced pork, nuts and coconut, egg yolk or other ingredients. Modern-day adaptations include mocha-flavoured moon cakes from Starbucks and ice-cream versions from Häagen-Dazs.

On 1 October 1949, Mao Zedong stood above Tiananmen Square and announced the birth of the People's Republic of China. The anniversary is celebrated with yet another week's break from work—which is scheduled, again, as a prime opportunity for the masses to go shopping.

shanghai's festivals

In early April, the folk fair at Longhua Temple features musicians, stilt-walkers, opera singers, jugglers, incense burning, Buddhist ceremonies, tchotchke vendors and snacks galore. The ten-day affair dates back to the Ming Dynasty, more than 400 years ago.

Shanghai Tourism Festival is held during September. Festivities include a parade, brush-painting and other cultural activities, performances by dance troupes and local bands on temporary outdoor stages, as well as huge sales.

In November and December, the Shanghai International Arts Festival features plays, recitals, ballets, operas, symphonies and other class-acts from around the world. Performances are staged at the Shanghai Grand Theatre and other auditoriums in the city.

For the Shanghai Biennale (during November in even-numbered years), the Shanghai Art Museum devotes itself to displaying fringe and avant-garde paintings, sculptures, videos, multi-media and installation works of local and overseas artists.

THIS PAGE: Longhua Temple hosts a folk fair featuring Buddhist ceremonies, incense burning and opera singing.
OPPOSITE: The Shanghai Biennale showcases artwork from local and overseas artists. Held mainly at the Shanghai Art Museum, smaller galleries participate and exhibit more experimental pieces.

...plays, recitals, ballets, operas, symphonies and other class-acts from around the world...

the original chic set

In the 1930s and 1940s, Shanghai was not only the country's economic powerhouse but also its artistic capital. While foreign cultures and influences were absent from most of China, Shanghai was enlivened by foreigners from throughout the world, who had brought their art forms and styles with them. The Western nations occupying and self-governing the foreign-concession territories provided relatively greater freedom of expression to people living within their boundaries. That lured painters, musicians, writers, dramatists, intellectuals, composers, directors and singers—both famed and struggling—from across China to migrate and move in. The mixture of cultural backgrounds and the atmosphere of openness and acceptance fuelled an explosion in the arts. Shanghai became China's undisputed centre for everything from book publishing and filmmaking to jazz and Chinese opera.

dark days

In 1949, the state took control of all arts institutions and outlets, including radio stations, opera companies, film studios and orchestras, and managed every aspect, such as budgets, salaries, programme schedules and ticket sales. It centralized China's most talented artists in Beijing. Foreigners either left or were expelled from the country. Art was no longer a means of creative expression or entertainment, but of propaganda and political education. Paintings, for instance, were to be done in Soviet-realist style, featuring tractors, factories, red-cheeked, square-jawed peasants, workers and soldiers, and Chairman Mao Zedong.

During the Cultural Revolution, anything classical or Western was to be disavowed, burned, destroyed or otherwise eradicated. Anyone owning, espousing or practising anything old or Western was to be at least denigrated, if not punished. Mao's wife, a former B-movie starlet, dictated what was politically correct, and for the entire decade, the public could watch only eight revolutionary performance pieces, which included *The Red Detachment of Women* ballet and the modern opera *Taking Tiger Mountain by Strategy*.

THIS PAGE: Mao memorabilia from the Cultural Revolution, an example of the dominating Soviet-realist style.

OPPOSITE: Artistic expression made a comeback in the late 1990s.

an artistic revival

As Shanghai began revamping its economy in the 1990s, it realized that it couldn't remain an artistic wasteland. The government began to build. The Shanghai Museum, which many overseas curators consider the world's finest museum of Chinese art, opened in 1996, followed two years later by the Shanghai Grand Theatre, the best performing arts venue in China. The new Oriental Art Centre in Pudong is state-of-the-art, and the city has building plans for a theatre specifically for long-running musical spectacles à la Broadway. Private capital has been an arts booster, too, with foreign and local entrepreneurs establishing galleries and jazz clubs. Exhibits and performances, though, must be approved by the state's cultural authorities, who still view the arts primarily as indoctrination tools and mirrors of China's values. The government's decisions and control can still be unpredictable; for example, a previously approved production of *The Vagina Monologues* in Shanghai was abruptly cancelled the day before it was to open.

The arts scene is less energetic than it was in the 1930s and isn't as inspired and creative as Beijing's, but Shanghai does have the hardware and infrastructure of a world-class arts capital. And there are enough plays, recitals and exhibit openings in Shanghai to occupy every night of the week.

As has happened with the economy, the arts sector has become more decentralized and privatized. Government funding has been cut, and arts organizations have become more independent.

Artists and exhibits from abroad are making Shanghai a regular stop. During the 2004–05 'Year of France in China' (which followed the previous 'Year of China in France'), Shanghai saw such treats as the baroque opera *Les Paladins*, the Lyon Opera's ballet company, and exhibits of legendary Cartier jewellery, French impressionist masterpieces and photographs by Robert Doisneau and Henri Cartier-Bresson. Over

THIS PAGE (FROM TOP): **The performing arts received a boost with the opening of the Shanghai Grand Theatre, the best in China; more and more artists are including Shanghai as a regular stop to showcase their work.**

OPPOSITE (FROM TOP): **Traditional-style screens at Xintiandi; the area around Xintiandi was given a breath of life when the popular complex of bars, restaurants, a museum and a park was developed.**

roughly the same period, luminaries including Yo-Yo Ma, Elton John, Vivienne Westwood, *The Phantom of the Opera*, Tan Dun, Stomp, Norah Jones, David Henry Hwang, Ice-T, Andy Lau and Seiji Ozawa came to visit and show themselves, too.

literature

Once upon a time, Shanghai was the literary and publishing centre of China. In the foreign enclaves, novelists and essayists were protected from the censorship of Chinese authorities. Chinese literary hits that were written or based in Shanghai from the 1920s to 1940s include Ba Jin's *Family* and Mao Dun's *Midnight*, both about the tension in Chinese families between Confucian doctrine and modern, liberal ideas. Lu Xun (1881–1936), considered the father of modern Chinese literature, wrote in a more familiar and colloquial Chinese style rather than in the ancient, classical Chinese that most of the public couldn't understand. Besides creating a vernacular prose, Lu made jabs at the Kuomintang and China's social problems in short stories such as *The True Story of Ah Q* and *Diary of a Madman*. Eileen Chang, who spent the last part of her life in the US, described the city's pulse and the often confining, downtrodden lives of women in *The Golden Lock* and other books.

In cooperation with the Hong Kong Literary Arts Festival, Shanghai stages a springtime literary festival that features talks by local and international award-winning authors, often on Asia-related themes.

chinese painting and calligraphy

Ink-brush painting and calligraphy are the most honoured of the traditional Chinese arts. They were among the essential skills expected of the scholarly class. Calligraphy comes in many styles, ranging from very square, formal characters to 'grass writing', a quick cursive whose characters can be hard to decipher. Paintings are thought to reflect the artist's values and frame of mind, and the most popular subject is nature (for example, animals, bamboo, pine trees, mountains, landscapes). Two of the most

famous brush painters based in Shanghai are Xu Beihong and Liu Haisu. (The latter is the focus of an art gallery in Shanghai).

A two-hour drive south of Shanghai, Jinshan is a centre of homey peasant paintings produced by the locals. The painters have not had any formal art education, but their artwork is full of cheery colours and the tiniest details from everyday life. They create pictures of rural and domestic bliss: a wedding parade of well-wishers and musicians, a bustling marketplace, a harvest, a household celebrating Chinese New Year, or simply a woman cooking dinner.

contemporary art

Modern art is in. Galleries are popping up throughout Shanghai, and exhibition previews and openings are prime occasions to see and be seen. The Shanghai Biennale, which gets international attention, showcases the latest and edgiest every two years. The city has two museums of modern art, the Duolun and the Zendai, along with arty districts such as Taikang Road and Moganshan.

Among the designer boutiques and trendy restaurants at Three on the Bund is the impressive Shanghai Gallery of Art. Dingy former factories and warehouses from the 1930s along Suzhou Creek have been overhauled and remodelled to hold design studios and galleries. Artists in Shanghai include Ding Yi, whose paintings almost resemble weaving; Zhou Tiehai, winner of a national contemporary art award; abstract painter Shen Fan; Wu Yiming, whose style is Impressionist-like; and photographers Gangfeng Wang and Yang Fudong.

Shanghai's government is determined to spread art to the masses who aren't museum- or gallery-goers. It takes a soft-pedal approach, installing public art that is mostly realistic and easily grasped. Among the art pieces dotting Shanghai are a cast of Rodin's *The Large Thinker*, a statue of Russian writer Alexander Pushkin, a pointy starfish-like sculpture commemorating an anti-government protest in 1925, Chen Yifei's humongous sundial, *Light of the East*, and several life-size depictions of ordinary lives in

THIS PAGE: Artists, designers and galleries are moving into Suzhou Creek's 1930s factories and warehouses.

OPPOSITE (FROM TOP): Shanghai Gallery of Art displays impressive art work; Wu Sa Memorial pays tribute to a 30 May 1925 student protest against foreign domination in Shanghai.

metal, such as a man sitting on a bench, a woman pushing a stroller and a saxophonist. In preparing to host the World Expo in 2010, the government plans to install around town 400 new creations by Chinese and foreign artists.

The most famous artist in Shanghai—perhaps the most renowned in contemporary China—was Chen Yifei. Chen, who died in 2005, was said to be a quintessential Shanghai artist because he turned art into a commercial goldmine. A painting of his fetched US$500,000 in 1997, which is still the highest price paid for a piece by a living Chinese artist. After studying painting in Shanghai, Chen had spent a decade in the US to study further and later work at tycoon Armand Hammer's gallery in New York. His portraits of young women of bygone days playing classical Chinese instruments and of Tibetans in ethnic dress, painted in a realist, Rembrandt-like style, were unexpected hits in the US and Hong Kong. By the time Chen returned to Shanghai in 1990, many of his contemporaries had turned to abstract or avant-garde styles, but Chen stuck to realism. He also launched a modelling agency, his own fashion label, a home furnishings store and *Shanghai Tatler*, a glossy magazine filled with paparazzi photographs of socialites. Chen, who wore imported Italian suits and bought real estate around town, was a proponent of his own bourgeois lifestyle. His goal, he said, was 'to bring aesthetics to Chinese society' and 'provide beauty to the people'.

musically minded

Shanghai, the home of China's first Western orchestra and first music school, has been a long-time lover of Western classical music. The Shanghai Symphony Orchestra was formed in 1879 as a band in the foreign concessions. It evolved into an orchestra and became known as the best in Asia. At first, its musicians were White Russians, Jews and other foreigners, but in the late 1930s, Chinese could join. The group has played in Carnegie Hall and is considered China's top symphony.

Other classical groups include the Shanghai Philharmonic Orchestra and the Shanghai National Music Orchestra. Performances are often held at the Shanghai

Grand Theatre and the historic Shanghai Concert Hall. The concert hall opened in 1930 as a theatre (it was nicknamed the 'Asian Roxy') but later was converted into a symphony hall. In 2004, the auditorium of baby blue with gilt trim was renovated.

Jazz's history in Shanghai is almost as long as classical music's. During the boisterous 1920s and 1930s, Shanghai was China's epicentre of jazz, where an estimated 500 jazz bands, composed of mainly Filipinos and Russians, played the clubs. Today the Peace Hotel's band, which includes a few septuagenarians who were in the band before 1949, pipes out New Orleans-style oldies. Musicians from the Philippines, the US, Europe and elsewhere come to play the fast-expanding jazz circuit of five-star hotel lounges and swank restaurants. One of the best-known Shanghai vocalists is Coco, a guy who often cross-dresses.

By comparison, rock, pop and alternative music first appeared in China only in the late 1980s, and home-grown music today is largely commercial and mainstream. The experimental scene suffers from a lack of sponsors, but is showing signs of growth. Local rock bands include The Honeys, Cold Fairyland, Bird on a Wire and Crystal Butterfly, and rappers include Bamboo Crew and Peng Peng. For now, the musicians who can fill Shanghai's sport stadiums are primarily from Taiwan, Hong Kong and Japan, like Coco Lee, Jay Chou, Jacky Cheung and L'Arc-en-Ciel.

Non-live music may well have a wider following than the live forms. Karaoke fans, who are especially faithful and serious, include middle-aged business types (who consider karaoke a perfect activity for entertaining clients) and younger sets. The newest brand of celebrities is DJs spinning techno, house, tribal, hip-hop or trance, and Shanghai clubs proudly trumpet their line-ups of local and visiting foreign DJs.

traditional performances

Acrobats in China have been twisting, balancing and hurtling themselves in unimaginable ways for 2,000 years. The acrobatic shows held regularly at Shanghai Centre Theatre and Shanghai Circus World are wowing audiences and are well

THIS PAGE: *Rehearsals at the Shanghai Grand Theatre.*

OPPOSITE: *Cotton Club and House of Blues & Jazz are two of the best jazz clubs in town.*

worth it. The eerie pretzel contortions, dizzying tightrope and gymnastic stunts and feats of breathtaking balance, strength and precision seem to defy laws of physics and nature. It's truly a sight to behold.

Chinese opera evolved from centuries of itinerant troupes blending and performing traditional ballads and dance. To the uninitiated, the opera's whirl of falsetto arias, acrobatics, martial arts, shrill music and heavily stylized choreography can be difficult to digest. Since the stage sets and props are minimal and the actors' movements often subtle yet highly symbolic, opera-goers must summon their imaginations. Storylines often trace Chinese historical events or legends.

More than 100 varieties of opera exist in China. The most famous is Beijing, which is heavy on the acrobatic manoeuvres, percussion and facial make-up. The painted faces of the actors indicate their type of role or character (for example, a black face signifies an honest official; a white nose belongs to a clown). Often the tales are about epic heroes. The mother of all Chinese opera—the oldest form of theatre in China—is Kunju. It originated in Kunshan, about an hour's drive from Shanghai, during the 16th century, and is for strict traditionalists. Compared to Beijing opera, Kunju is slower-paced and more lyrical. The music, often led by a flute, is more melodic. The most famous Kunju opera is *The Peony Pavilion*, an erotic love story of a young maiden and a young scholar that easily stretches longer than 20 hours. Only a handful of Kunju companies remain in China, the best being the Shanghai Kun Opera Troupe.

Other opera varieties native to the Shanghai area are Huju, which is sung in the Shanghainese dialect, and Yueju from Zhejiang, which was born around the 1920s and which commonly has women filling all of the roles in tragic love tales.

theatre

Contemporary theatre is flourishing in Shanghai. Drama enthusiasts normally have their pick of plays; one recent week, the offerings included the Chinese hit comedy *The House of 72 Tenants*, an adaptation of Neil Simon's *The Last of the Red-Hot Lovers*,

two plays exploring the meaning of life and love in a complex, modern city, and Hans Christian Andersen's *The Little Match Girl* and *The Ugly Duckling*. Theatre from abroad comes to Shanghai regularly; English actors, for instance, have performed *Othello* and a show based on *The Merchant of Venice*.

During the past few years, China has allowed Western producers to bring in a smattering of musical extravaganzas including *Cats* and *The Phantom of the Opera*. Shanghai's government, now anxious to create a local musical-theatre industry, is collaborating with British impresario Cameron Mackintosh to develop Mandarin-language versions of *Les Miserables* and other crowd-pleasers.

dance

White Russian émigrés brought ballet to Shanghai in the 1920s. During the Cultural Revolution, the delicate dance form was revolutionized, literally. The two ballets that were approved for performance featured battles against feudalism, fascism and oppression. Ballerinas who had spent years dancing to resemble gentle, lithe swans reappeared as rifle-toting peasants and soldiers with glares of hatred, clenched jaws and fists and bright red pointé shoes.

These days, the Shanghai Ballet repertoire contains Russian classics, Chinese revolutionary or proletarian ballets and some modern choreography.

Other dance groups include the Shanghai Song and Dance Ensemble and Jin Xing's eponymous troupe. Jin Xing, the boldest choreographer in Shanghai, if not China, is a transsexual who was formerly a People's Liberation Army officer. Her renown comes as much from her high-publicity sex change as from her dance talent. But her young Jin Xing Dance Theatre has already partnered with foreign dancers and taken on complex projects such as interpreting the dark *Carmina Burana* symphony.

Dance in Shanghai is not only a spectator sport. Clubs and restaurants host weekly salsa and swing lessons. Teams of middle-aged and elderly women regularly converge in public for dance-cum-exercise, twirling red fans as they step, swivel and

THIS PAGE (FROM TOP): Contemporary choreography combining acrobatics and dance; the visual spectacle of Shanghai Tango, performed in Shanghai's Grand Theatre.

OPPOSITE (FROM TOP): The Beijing Kunju Opera troupe performing in Shanghai; the Cultural Revolution-era play Shajiabang, staged by the Shanghai Beijing Opera Troupe.

wriggle in practised synchronicity. At dusk, parks in Xujiahui and near the US Consulate are transformed into outdoor ballrooms of waltzing, foxtrotting, and sashaying Shanghainese. They may like to watch other people dance, but Shanghainese love doing it themselves too.

the big screen

Shanghai boasts many cinematic firsts. China's first cinema opened in Shanghai in 1908. The first China-produced film was made in Shanghai. By 1930 there were more than 35 movie theatres and 140 film companies in the city. Opening nights of movies were glittery affairs. Greta Garbo, Marlene Dietrich, Gregory Peck, and Katharine Hepburn were as familiar to the public as Chinese stars Ruan Lingyu ('China's Garbo'), Zhou Xuan, Zhao Dan and Butterfly Wu were.

In the 1980s, after decades of making ideological propaganda, China's film industry began a much-needed turnaround. The Beijing Film Academy produced its first batch of graduates since the Cultural Revolution, which included Zhang Yimou and Chen Kaige. Zhang garnered international acclaim for his films *Red Sorghum*, *Ju Dou* and *Raise the Red Lantern*, even though some of them were initially banned in China.

Partly because Shanghai was left with insufficient resources for many years (as dictated by the central government), the city has yet to regain its 1930s title as 'China's Hollywood'. Shanghai has been the backdrop for foreign productions such as *The Great Raid*, *Code 46* and *Ultraviolet*, but it doesn't want to build a reputation tied to thrillers and action flicks alone. Thus the Shanghai Film Group Corporation has been courting respected international filmmakers to shoot other genres in Shanghai. It and Merchant Ivory Productions agreed to co-produce *The White Countess*, and the Merchant Ivory team in 2004 spent three months shooting the film, which is set in 1937 Shanghai. That was followed by the filming of *Perhaps Love*, China's first movie musical in 30 years, whose producers, cast and crew are from the US, Hong Kong, Japan, India and China.

THIS PAGE: *Shanghai has several multi-screen cinemas attached to shopping malls.*
OPPOSITE: *Performance of the ballet adaptation of Zhang Yimou's film, 'Raise the Red Lantern', was staged at the Shanghai Grand Theatre.*

They may like to watch other people dance, but Shanghainese love doing it themselves too.

the way the land lies

Shanghai wouldn't be Shanghai if it weren't for water. In its earliest incarnation, Shanghai was a fishing hamlet. Near the Yangzi estuary, which hooked up to a network of waterways across the region, and near the Pacific Ocean, its prime location destined it to become a bustling port.

Water still defines the metropolis today. The Huangpu River, the city's vital link to the Yangzi River and to the sea, cuts Shanghai proper into two parts with apt names: Puxi (literally meaning 'west of the Huangpu') and Pudong ('east of the Huangpu'). Suzhou Creek, which runs east–west, separates a northern swathe from the rest of the city. Old canals and creeks formed some of the boundaries of neighbourhoods and the foreign concessions during the early 20th century; they have since been filled in and are now busy arterial roads, but they still help demarcate the present districts of Shanghai municipality.

the bund

More than anything or anywhere else, this majestic waterfront of massive architecture trumpets 'Shanghai!' The city's top visitor attraction, the jaw-dropping, 2-km (1.2 miles)-long Bund is a snapshot of the foreign-concession era, when Britain and other Western nations won commerce and occupation rights in Shanghai by defeating China in the Opium Wars. The Bund became their trading, financial and shipping hub, where the important banks, hotels and private clubs built dramatic European-style structures for themselves.

'Bund' is a term taken from British India, an adaptation of the Hindi word band, meaning 'embankment'. Originally a soggy path for towing barges, the Huangpu's shore had to be filled in and fortified before it could accommodate buildings and jetties. Like Venice, Shanghai is gradually sinking, and the raised promenade presently along the Bund serves as a dyke. (The Huangpu is now higher than downtown's street level.) The Chinese name for the Bund is Waitan, or 'outside beach'.

THIS PAGE (FROM TOP): China's flag flies from the former headquarters of foreign banks and shipping companies; the colonial looking No. 18 was built in 1923.

OPPOSITE: The historic Bund is stately by day and glamorous by night.

Most of the two dozen stately Bund buildings are neoclassical in style and about half were erected in the 1920s. The Hong Kong and Shanghai Bank wanted its building at No. 12 to dominate the Bund. It did—and still does. Designed by British architectural firm Palmer and Turner, it was finished in 1923. Today, it is occupied by the Pudong Development Bank. The dome-crowned exterior is grand, but be sure to duck inside for the intricate ceiling mosaics and the regal marble columns and flooring. There's more marble inside the finely crafted elevators. Ride them to the second-floor coffee shop, which has an airy terrace in the building's centre. The two Western-style bronze lions guarding the entrance (replicas of the originals) are considered good luck; Chinese have always liked to rub their noses.

Palmer and Turner's work dominates the Bund. Next door to the bank, the 1927 Customs House is also one of their buildings, distinguished by its towering clock, fondly known as 'Big Ching'. The firm also designed the 1929 Cathay Hotel (now the Peace Hotel) and the two bank buildings just north of it. The Cathay, owned by magnate Sir Victor Sassoon, had a guest register that included Charlie Chaplin, George Bernard Shaw and Noël Coward, who wrote *Private Lives* during one stay. Filmmakers such as Spielberg and Merchant and Ivory have used the Art Deco jewel to recreate the aura of the 1930s.

American International Assurance is back at No. 17, which it had leased before 1949; it is the only company that has returned to its pre-revolution premises in Shanghai. The Palmer-and-Turner-created insurance company headquarters at No. 3 and neoclassical bank at No. 18 have undergone restoration and remodelling, and recently reopened with fine dining, posh bars, designer boutiques and art exhibition space. Some of the other Bund buildings are slated for renovation, some are empty and others house government offices and state-owned companies.

To see the rest of Puxi, head west. Leading off from the Bund, Nanjing Road has been China's most renowned shopping street for eight decades. It boasts venerable food and department stores, Art Deco buildings from the 1920s and 1930s, and throngs of tourists.

people's square

Besides being the geographical centre of Shanghai, People's Square has a concentration of the finest of the municipality's modern showpieces. The monuments of civic and architectural pride were all built during the 1990s. At the northwest edge of the square, the Shanghai Grand Theatre presents the biggest acts in dance, music, opera and drama, at ticket prices comparable to New York's and London's. It gets its nickname, 'Crystal Palace', from its sparkling illumination at night.

The Shanghai Museum, perhaps the world's finest museum of Chinese art, is a Chinese historian's or art lover's dream. Its treasure troves of ancient bronzes, sculpture, ceramics, painting, calligraphy, jade and furniture are comprehensive and thoughtfully presented. It also has a gallery with art and costumes of China's 56 ethnic minorities. The building itself has the shape of an ancient bronze cooking pot or incense burner. The circular upper part and square lower part are also said to be allusions to the traditional belief that heaven is round and the Earth is square.

THIS PAGE: *People's Square, as viewed from the roof of the Shanghai Art Museum.*

OPPOSITE: (ANTI-CLOCKWISE FROM TOP): *No. 12, the queen of the Bund, has magnificent mosaics inside and bronze lions guarding outside; the venerable Peace Hotel.*

For a peek into the future, head to the northeast end of People's Square. At the sleek, white Urban Planning Exhibition Hall, a clock ticks down to 2010, when the World Expo hits town. Inside, a 500-sq-m (5,380-sq-ft) scale model reveals the Shanghai that Expo visitors should expect to see.

The streets encircling People's Square and the adjacent People's Park trace what was a horse racecourse before 1949. The former clubhouse of the Shanghai Racing Club is now home to the Shanghai Art Museum.

nanshi, the old city

With its crammed alleyways, poles of hanging laundry and small shops selling steamed buns, Shaoxing wine, and grain, Nanshi ('southern city') is the most traditionally Chinese part of Shanghai. It is the oldest part, too, the site of what was a fishing village around the 11th century. Its circular perimeter is where a wall and moat once stood to protect the city against Japanese pirates. During the concession era, Shanghainese were initially limited to living in Nanshi. But as more Chinese fled the insurgency battles in outlying provinces and sought sanctuary in Shanghai's policed foreign enclaves, Western developers foresaw their fortunes in erecting housing for Chinese in the concession districts.

At the northern end of the Old City is Yuyuan Gardens, Shanghai's foremost example of classical Chinese garden design. Built by a 16th-century Ming official, the gardens' pavilions, fish ponds, rockery and landscaping have been damaged and restored several times. The postcard-perfect Mid-Lake Pavilion Teahouse next door, which sits in the middle of a lake, has had Queen Elizabeth II and Bill Clinton over for tea. Surrounding the gardens is a bazaar of hundreds of speciality shops and food stands in Ming-style buildings.

Other interesting places in the Old City: Xiaotaoyuan (Peach Orchard) Mosque; Confucius Temple; and Baiyun (White Cloud) Taoist Temple. Fangbang Road, which was once a canal, has dealers selling antiques, curios and Cultural Revolution

THIS PAGE: Shanghai Museum's symbolic shape resembles an ancient pot or incense burner.

OPPOSITE (FROM LEFT): Yuyuan Gardens glow at night; looking up at its swooping traditional roofs.

paraphernalia. Even more antiques—some truly old, most not—are at the Dongtai Road Antiques Market, which is situated just west of the Old City.

fuxing park + luwan

About 10 sq km (4 sq miles) in all, the French Concession started from the southern end of the Bund, skirted around Nanshi and stretched west across today's Luwan district. Its northern boundary (separating it from the International Settlement) was a creek that was later filled in to become a road (present-day Yan An Road). As of the 1930s, the French were a minority of the enclave's residents. But wandering the avenues today, you can still sense the feeling of a grand European city.

As the heart of the former French quarter, the area around Fuxing Park has many especially graceful and historically noteworthy houses and hotels. Fuxing Park, created by the French in 1909 and then called 'French Park', is one of Shanghai's most pleasant public gardens. The verdant grounds, which have statues of Marx and Engels, draw daily Chinese exercisers, busying themselves with tai chi, dancing, martial arts, walking and stretching.

East of the park is Xintiandi ('New Heaven and Earth'), one of the most happening spots in Shanghai. Developed by a Hong Kong company, the trendy complex shifted the shikumen from its traditional residential duty to a high-end commercial role. Inside Xintiandi's recreated shikumen shells are all manner of restaurants, bars and clothing and gift boutiques, next to a man-made lake. A block away is the restored shikumen where Chinese Communist Party delegates, including Mao Zedong, secretly held their first congress, in 1921.

Directly west of Fuxing Park is a home of Sun Yatsen, the father of modern China, who founded the Kuomintang party and in 1911, China's first republic. Down the road is a Spanish-style villa where former premier Zhou Enlai once lived.

Much grander in scale is the former Morriss Estate, a spread of lawns and villas with stained glass windows built by a British magnate, who also owned the

THIS PAGE (FROM TOP): Curios hanging at a street market; Xintiandi's restored stone doorways and façades.

OPPOSITE (FROM TOP): The Morriss Estate now houses Face Bar and other establishments; out for a stroll in the former French Concession.

Canidrome dog racetrack next door. The compound now contains Face Bar and Ruijin Guesthouse; the Canidrome is home to a lively flower market.

On opposite sides of Maoming Road are two hotels full of history. The Okura Garden Hotel was originally Cercle Sportif Francaise (the French Club), one of Shanghai's poshest clubs, outfitted with tennis courts and an indoor pool. It became one of Mao Zedong's favourite places to stay while in Shanghai. Pop inside to see the luscious marble, columns with nudes and the ballroom's stained-glass. Across the street, the Art Deco Jinjiang Hotel opened in 1929. There, in 1972, Richard Nixon and Zhou Enlai signed the Shanghai Communiqué, bringing détente to US–China relations.

If you need a commercial break, Huaihai Road is the place where stylish Shanghai shops. The long road's central section is chock-a-block with department stores, shopping plazas and elaborate wedding photo salons, where brides can select from racks and racks of flouncy gowns and get dolled up for photo sessions with the groom. For shopping of a different nature, stop by Xiangyang Fashion Market, at Xiangyang

and Huaihai. Stalls here are stuffed with clothes, table linen, purses, backpacks, watches, jewellery, silk and sunglasses. Most of the products labelled with brand-names are knock-offs, but some of them are the real thing, that fell off the back of a truck.

There are relatively peaceful and arty avenues to wind down after a bout of Xiangyang bargaining. Taikang Road is a colony of galleries, artists' and designers' studios and home décor shops, some in renovated factories. Shaanxi Road is stocked with more home furnishings and tasteful accessories. Shaoxing Road offers galleries with artwork and some bookshops/reading rooms. All of the streets have cafes where you're welcome to lounge.

huaihai + hengshan

Sublime old mansions with gardens, broad avenues, greenery and comparative tranquillity make the Huaihai–Hengshan area the neighbourhood of choice. As part of the former French Concession, it is dotted with French-planted plane trees that have formed canopies over the boulevards, making the territory ideal for walks.

At Huaihai and Urumqi, diplomacy converges: the US and Iranian consulates and the French and Japanese consul-generals' homes are all within a one-block radius. (The German consul's home is a couple of blocks away.) Next to the Japan consul's residence is the white-tile Shanghai Library, appropriately fronted by a cast of Rodin's *The Large Thinker*.

Also on Huaihai is a villa and lush yard where Soong Chingling lived after her husband, Sun Yatsen, died. The home has a display of photos and documents about the illustrious Soong family, whose patriarch, Charlie Soong, was educated in the US and became a

Methodist. He returned to Shanghai and befriended Sun Yatsen. His daughters, all of whom were sent to the US for college, married well: the eldest, Ailing, married the scion of a banking family, who became a finance minister of the Kuomintang government; Meiling wed Chiang Kaishek, the Kuomintang head who fought the Communists unsuccessfully and fled to Taiwan in 1949; Chingling married Sun. Only the youngest stayed in China after the Communist victory. Mainland Chinese frequently say that Ailing loved money, Meiling loved power, and Chingling loved China.

The country's second-oldest university, Jiaotong, is on Huashan Road. It's known for its science and engineering brains. Although the elite neighbourhood is sedate overall, Hengshan Road is a nocturnal animal. Come night-time, young Chinese and foreigners hop from English pub to Chinese teahouse to pulsating disco. Clusters of friends stroll and strut. Dining options range from white-tablecloth Continental cuisine in a Soong-family villa to grilled lamb kebabs from a Uighur sidewalk vendor. The sounds of live Chinese rap and Filipino cover bands drift from tiny clubs.

An entirely different genus of nightlife emerges at Xujiahui Park. At dusk, Shanghainese ballroom-dance to Chinese orchestral music broadcast over tinny loudspeakers. The nightly session draws all ages and types—retirees who're lifetime waltzers, giggling women, middle-aged couples in pyjamas, toddlers, and surly chain-smokers.

xujiahui

In contrast to the general serenity of Huaihai and Hengshan, Xujiahui is a sensory explosion. Neon-lit mega-malls have food, movies, video game parlours, karaoke, and shopping, shopping, shopping all under one roof. The road intersections look like the legs of a mutant octopus. People with bullhorns or dressed as robots or cartoon characters talk up the hot sales. On the western edge of what was the French Concession, Xujiahui looks all new.

But not quite. Standing next to the shopping frenzy is the red-brick Xujiahui Cathedral, which was built in 1906 as St. Ignatius Cathedral. Its Gothic towers

THIS PAGE (FROM TOP): Sun Yatsen, the father of modern China, is revered by the Communists and Kuomintang alike; the mansions of Shanghai offer great entertainment venues. OPPOSITE: One of Sun Yatsen's former villas.

were restored after they were chopped off by Red Guards during the Cultural Revolution. At Christmas and Easter services the cathedral has standing room only.

Shanghai's largest Catholic church owes its existence to Matteo Ricci's assistant and pupil, Xu Guangqi (Paul Xu), who was born in the area in 1562. Xu was the first Ming court official to convert to Christianity. He bequeathed his family land to establish a Jesuit community, which eventually built a monastery, library, publishing house, orphanage, meteorological observatory and the cathedral. (Only a few of the structures remain today.) Xujiahui ('the Xu family residence') is named after him.

Older still are the Longhua Temple and Pagoda in southwest Shanghai. The temple, the city's biggest, has five halls with Buddhist statues dating from the Qing Dynasty, plus a bell and a drum tower. The picturesque eight-sided, seven-storey pagoda of brick and wood has gone through several restorations since it was first built in the 10th century. Longhua's Chinese New Year fair is not to be missed. Next to the temple, a park and cemetery—previously the site of a Kuomintang prison—memorialize the White Terror, the Kuomintang's mass round-up and slaughter of Shanghai Communists in 1927.

hongqiao + gubei

A little more than a decade ago it was farmland, but now Hongqiao and Gubei are where trade fairs meet suburbia. Several of Shanghai's exhibition centres are located here, their halls often staging a few shows simultaneously. Gubei, a semi-planned community catering to expatriate families, was Shanghai's first foreign enclave after 1949. It developed quickly in the early 1990s, its gated complexes evoking classical splendour with names like 'Mandarine City' and 'Gold Lion' and larger-than-life statues of horses and generic Greek and Roman figures. Today, Gubei has large congregations of Japanese, Taiwanese and Korean expatriates.

Shanghai's first Carrefour, the French version of Wal-Mart, opened here. But this area also has the best selection of antique furniture (and replicas) in Shanghai. Shops and warehouses are clumped along Hongqiao, Wuzhong and Hongxu roads.

THIS PAGE (FROM TOP): Shanghai's largest Catholic church; the octagonal, 44-m (144-ft)-tall Longhua Pagoda.
OPPOSITE: Lights and action along Nanjing Road.

Off Hongqiao Road is Soong Chingling's mausoleum, which is marked by a white marble statue of her. On the grounds is also a 'foreigners' tomb area', which was set up in 1909 as the International Cemetery. It has tombstones of a few of pre-1949 Shanghai's wealthiest foreigners, such as the Sephardic Jewish leader Elly Kadoorie, whose extravagant and accurately named Marble Hall is now used as an arts centre for gifted children.

jing'an

Though named after its ancient temple, the Jing'An district is a commercial hub of ultra-glossy shopping emporiums, five-star hotels, prestigious office towers and deluxe service apartments. This section of Nanjing Road is lined with Westgate Mall, CITIC Square, Plaza 66 and Sogo Shopping Plaza offering Tiffany, Chanel, Ferragamo, Gaultier, Tod's, Cartier and the like, as well as a Starbucks coffee shop on every block. A city landmark that even the greenest cabbies know is Shanghai Centre, an expat-tailored and self-contained residential-business complex with restaurants, medical clinics, day-care, a gym, bank and grocery and yes, a Starbucks. The Shanghai Centre Theatre's acrobatics show dazzles. (It's important to note that cabbies know the Centre as Bo-te-man, after the Portman Ritz-Carlton Hotel in its centre.)

Opposite the Shanghai Centre and the other high-rises of modernity is an attention-grabbing throwback, the Shanghai Exhibition Centre. Topped by a 106-m (347-ft) gold-plated steeple and a Communist star, the striking exhibition

monolith is a testament to 1950s Sino–Soviet unity—and looks it, too. Its walls are often draped with red banners advertising the shows inside.

Many people are momentarily distracted by the sight of the Exhibition Centre, but they do triple-takes at the witch's fantasy castle at Shaanxi and Yan An roads. It's actually a Gothic mansion built in 1936 by Swedish shipping tycoon Eric Moller, outfitted with wood from Sweden and steeples. For many years it was the Communist Youth League's headquarters, but it is now a boutique hotel.

Jing'An Temple, built along Suzhou Creek in 247, has the longest history of any temple in the city, and is actually older than Shanghai itself. It was moved to its present location in the 13th century. Before 1949, it was one of the richest temples in Shanghai, run by a popular abbot who had a wife, seven concubines and a White Russian bodyguard. During the Cultural Revolution, the temple was turned into a plastics factory and much of its architecture and décor was destroyed. It has since undergone several renovation jobs and has been largely encircled by new shopping malls.

Almost directly north of Jing'An Temple is Jade Buddha Temple, which survived the Cultural Revolution intact when its monks locked the doors and covered them with pictures of Chairman Mao. The complex, completed in 1918, is relatively new. Its two jade Buddhas (2-m (6.6 ft) and 1-m (3.2 ft) high) were carved in Burma and brought to Shanghai in the 1880s by a Chinese pilgrim.

hongkou + north shanghai

The area north of Suzhou Creek is gritty, rather worn down and heavily Chinese—and has been so for decades. It became the American Settlement in 1854 and later merged with the British concession to form the International Settlement. In Shanghai's tortuous history of the early 20th century, it was this section of the city that suffered most. Hongkou had a large Japanese community in the 1920s, as well as Dickensian factories and slums. In 1931, more than 10,000 civilians in the district were killed in Sino-Japanese cross-fire, and much of the area was razed by Japanese bombs.

THIS PAGE (FROM TOP): The Shanghai Exhibition Centre; the doors of the Jade Buddha Temple that survived the Cultural Revolution.
OPPOSITE: **Monks at Jade Buddha Temple.**

During World War II, northern Shanghai was where the Japanese occupying forces were based—and where they corralled Jewish refugees into a ghetto. The steel Waibaidu Bridge spanning Suzhou Creek was the boundary between the Japanese-controlled territory and the International Settlement; on one end, it was patrolled by Japanese troops and on the other, by Britain's Sikh-Indian guards.

Sephardic Jews who came to Shanghai in the last half of the 19th century made their fortunes from opium, trading, warehousing, property and other ventures, and funded Jewish hospitals, clubs, schools and seven synagogues. Russian Jews escaping anti-Jewish pogroms came next, and then Jews from across Europe, fleeing the Nazis.

Shanghai required no visas, and between 1937 and 1939, some 30,000 Jewish refugees flooded into Shanghai. Labelling them as 'stateless persons', the Japanese crammed the refugees into 20 square blocks of Hongkou, where they lived alongside poor Chinese. Fortunately Ohel Moishe Synagogue, built in 1927, was within the boundaries. The earlier-arriving Jewish families were by now established and wealthy, such as the Sassoons, the Kadoories and the Hardoons, and were able to help the wartime refugees survive.

Hongkou's most famous resident was Lu Xun, a critic of Confucian culture and social injustices and the creator of a modern style of Chinese prose. The Communists consider him a hero, though he never joined the Party. His former house, a museum and a park with his tomb are all situated next to each other in Hongkou.

The father of Chinese vernacular literature is also among the local literati honoured with bronze statues on Duolun Cultural Street. Recently refurbished, the Duolun pedestrian avenue has tidy brick homes, galleries, curio shops, teahouses and the Duolun Museum of Modern Art.

Another section experiencing a renaissance is Moganshan Road along Suzhou Creek. There, old dilapidated warehouses have been remodelled into contemporary art galleries showcasing work of up-and-coming popular artists. Some have also been rented out as venues for hip parties.

THIS PAGE: A contemporary art piece on display.
OPPOSITE: The gritty Suzhou Creek area is undergoing some gentrification and is now a hub for the city's contemporary art galleries.

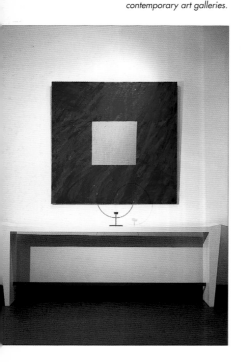

...pedestrian avenue has tidy brick homes, galleries, curio shops, teahouses...

88 Xintiandi

2002 saw the completion of Xintiandi, a creation inspired by Hong Kong and mainland China-based developers, Shui On Group. The sprawls of rundown Shikumen homes (traditional Shanghai housing) were restored, new buildings erected and an urban tourist attraction created. Located in the centre of the city it is instilled with the cultural and historical legacies of Shanghai, seen through the beautifully restored buildings and local museum. However, its main attraction is the smart boutiques, stylish restaurants and numerous cafés and bars that have gathered here, along with tourists, business travellers, expatriates and locals. Part of the development includes 88 Xintiandi, a luxury boutique hotel that has all the trappings of its urban chic surroundings.

There are 53 residences all designed to an exceptional level of quality and taste. Complete with their own kitchen area and amenities, the residence suites at 88 Xintiandi provide for the rare and often longed for opportunity of a night in. A huge, regal desk can combine as a cosy dining area, creating the ultimate in home comforts.

...a luxury boutique hotel that has all the trappings of its urban chic surroundings.

Of course, for a night on the sofa or a quick reprieve between a busy day and hectic night, each residence has its own sitting room complete with a flat-screen TV and DVD. Enormous double beds are tucked into custom-made alcoves, and the attractive muslin floating down from all sides not only keeps the mosquitoes away but adds to the overall sense of lightness and serenity. Chinese and South-East Asian furniture and accessories elegantly fill the room and their contrast with the modern simplicity of the decoration is striking. Every room has a balcony overlooking the plaza of Xintiandi or the Taipingqiao Lake and Park.

The hotel has a small restaurant dominated by a beautiful terrace, with wooden decking and stylish metal tables and chairs, overlooking the lake. Facilities include an inviting indoor swimming pool with sauna, steam room and Jacuzzi as well as a fitness centre.

With abundant shopping and dining surrounding 88 Xintiandi, it's a stone's throw away from a good night out. The careful design of the building, though, blankets the sounds of Shanghai's 24-hour partying so you can enjoy your own night of bliss. Just minutes by taxi from People's Square, the famous shopping hub on Nanjing Road and the stunning panorama of the Bund, 88 Xintiandi is the ultimate boutique choice for luxury, comfort and convenience.

THIS PAGE: The colour scheme and soft natural tones featured throughout the hotel provide pure comfort and tranquillity.

OPPOSITE (FROM TOP): The design radiates elegance and a touch of Shanghai's historical legacy; the luxurious beds are tucked into custom-made alcoves.

FACTS		
ROOMS	53	
FOOD	Villa du Lac	
DRINK	Villa du Lac	
FEATURES	indoor pool • gym • sauna • mini-kitchen	
NEARBY	Xintiandi • the Bund	
CONTACT	380 Huang Pi Nan Road, Shanghai, 200021 • telephone: +86.21.5383 8833 • facsimile: +86.21.5383 8877 • email: inquiry@88xintiandi.com • website: www.88xintiandi.com	

PHOTOGRAPHS COURTESY OF 88 XINTIANDI.

Four Seasons Hotel Shanghai

THIS PAGE: As well as the spa, the indoor pool is one of the hotel's great facilities.

OPPOSITE (FROM LEFT): The rooms are dotted with Chinese touches, reminding you of the city outside, the deluxe room is just one example; the stylish Jazz 37 where hotel guests can relax with a cocktail.

The first Four Seasons Hotel to be established in mainland China opened in Shanghai in 2002. Situated between Nanjing Road and Huaihai Road—the city's shopping and entertainment hub—Four Seasons Hotel Shanghai is an ideal location for exploring the city.

Scaling 37 floors, Four Seasons Hotel Shanghai comprises 439 luxurious guest rooms. The striking lobby area is dominated by huge palm trees, elegant furniture and warmth emanates from the huge sandy stonewalls. The rooms are designed with comfort in mind and each one benefits from a full-size sitting room, enormous beds and all the latest technology. Each is decorated in rich sumptuous colours, and the oversized furniture accentuates the feeling of pure comfort and homely reassurance.

The wealth of pampering options available include a fully-equipped spa where guests can completely re-balance and revitalize before stepping out into the city. After relaxing in the sauna or steam room

...oversized furniture accentuates the feeling of warmth and homely reassurance.

and the plunge pools, spa guests can choose from the extensive menu of relaxing and invigorating treatments. Massages range from Swedish to Sports to more traditional Chinese therapies such as acupressure and reflexology. For a little light activity, the indoor pool is adjoined to a stunning and spacious outdoor terrace—a welcome luxury in Shanghai.

With four restaurants and two bars, there's a huge diversity of food and entertainment available at Four Seasons Hotel

Shanghai. Si Ji Xuan, focused around an enormous aquarium, offers well-loved Cantonese and Shanghainese specialities. Shintaro serves Japanese-influenced cuisine from its open-style kitchen, and features a sociable seated counter and a private tatami room for those special occasions. For Western fare, the relaxed Steak House offers the chance to indulge in some prime beef whilst the Café Studio serves a blend of Italian cuisine with Asian flavour. A busy, street-level restaurant, Café Studio promotes local artists

and displays pieces of art along its walls for everyone to enjoy. The champagne brunch on Sundays is highly recommended.

With international renown, exemplary service and such variety, Four Seasons Hotel Shanghai well deserves its reputation as one of the foremost hotels in the world. Situated in a city that is constantly aiming for the tallest building, the fastest train or the highest bar, the magnificent scale of this hotel means it is more than able to stand up to Shanghai's grand aspirations.

FACTS		
ROOMS	439	
FOOD	Café Studio: blend of Italian and Asian • Shintaro: Japanese • Si Ji Xuan: Cantonese and Shanghainese • Steak House: Western	
DRINK	Jazz 37 • Lobby Lounge • pool terrace	
FEATURES	indoor pool • fitness centre • spa • business centre	
NEARBY	People's Square • Nanjing Road	
CONTACT	500 Weihai Road, Shanghai, 200041 • telephone: +86.21.6256 8888 • facsimile: +86.21.6256 5678 • website: www.fourseasons.com/shanghai	

PHOTOGRAPHS COURTESY OF FOUR SEASONS HOTEL SHANGHAI.

JW Marriott Hotel Shanghai

THIS PAGE (FROM TOP): The lobby is
an impressive welcome;
the indoor heated swimming
pool is just next to an outdoor
pool and the luxurious terrace
overlooking Nanjing Road.
OPPOSITE (FROM TOP): The Chairman
Suite, the only one in the hotel,
displays the impeccable style
and décor of the hotel;
the Wan Hao Chinese
restaurant offers Cantonese
cuisine in a stunning setting.

With a height of over 280 m (920 ft), Tomorrow Square stands as the tallest hotel building in Puxi. Its futuristic style and sleek lines make it an eye-catching landmark in Shanghai's crowded skyline and it's here, in this dominant and prestigious building, that the first JW Marriott Hotel opened in mainland China, in October 2003.

Located on Nanjing Road, Tomorrow Square sits in the middle of Shanghai's shopping and commercial centre. Adjacent to People's Square and People's Park, the hotel is within easy walking distance of the Bund and Xintiandi. Situated in the top 20 floors, the rooms offer breathtaking views of the city below. They are designed for luxurious comfort with rich silk textured walls, light airy duvets and all the latest in technology. Mahogany tea chests, jade ceramics and other Chinese artefacts add to the elegance and Oriental style. The bathrooms are ultra-modern and some are focused around huge, spectacular windows. With marble baths, separate power-jet showers and heated mirrors, they provide the ultimate treats that come with five-star living.

The hotel boasts two swimming pools. The heated indoor pool with its glass and metal structure provides an impressive setting. Outside, wooden decks and sun loungers surround the water. There is also the Mandara Spa—Asia's leading spa operator—to provide beauty and body treatments.

The substantial choice of restaurants are all situated on the upper floors of Tomorrow Square, they share the incredible, 360° views of the city. Sunday brunch is a popular activity in Shanghai and to experience it in style, try the Marriott Café or JW's California Grill. Both offer a free flow of champagne and an overwhelming choice at their buffets, from traditional breakfasts of eggs and bacon to pizza, from beef wellington to peking duck.

Wan Hao is a stunning, contemporary restaurant with sleek lacquer booths and gold textured walls showcasing traditional

Cantonese cuisine. JW's California Grill offers inspired American and Asian creations while JW's Lounge provides a colourful ambience for live entertainment and a bar menu including 60 concoctions of martini.

For a break from the glamour and excitement of the city, JW Marriott Hotel Shanghai offers the definitive resting spot in the world's highest library. Here you can browse through the collection of 1,500 books or ask staff to open up the rooftop terraces to enjoy a rare moment of solitude.

PHOTOGRAPHS COURTESY OF JW MARRIOTT HOTEL SHANGHAI.

FACTS

ROOMS	342
FOOD	Wan Hao • JW's California Grill • Marriott Café
DRINK	JW's Lounge • Lobby Lounge
FEATURES	indoor and outdoor pool • health club • 24-hour gym • Mandara Spa • 24-hour business centre • limousine service
NEARBY	People's Square • Xintiandi • Nanjing Pedestrian Walk • the Bund
CONTACT	JW Marriott Hotel Shanghai at Tomorrow Square, 399 Nanjing West Road, Shanghai, 200003 • telephone: +86.21.5359 4969 • facsimile: +86.21.6375 5988 • email: mhrs.shajw.reservations@marriotthotels.com • website: www.marriotthotels.com/shajw

The Westin Shanghai

Situated inside the prestigious Bund Centre, with a dramatic rooftop lotus lighting up the Shanghai night, there's no chance of losing your way back to the Westin Hotel. In the heart of Shanghai's most cosmopolitan district, close to the city's commercial, cultural and shopping hubs, it's a five-minute stroll to the elegant waterfront of the Bund and the bustling lanes of the Old City and an easy walk to People's Square and the popular shopping hub of Nanjing Road.

The impressive architecture continues inside in the form of a grand atrium lobby where tall palm trees strive to reach the sun pouring through the glass roof four floors above. A striking cantilevered glass staircase inlaid with delicate rice paper and beautiful soft-glow lighting welcomes you into the lobby.

The modern guestrooms exude a tasteful luxury and provide plenty of high-tech convenience and comfort. Their signature 'Heavenly Bed' is vast and electronically operated controls ensure a peaceful night. A comfortable sofa and armchair create a cosy living area to make the most of the flat-screen television and DVD. In the bathroom the 'rainforest' shower and marble bath provide both invigorating rejuvenation and deep, soothing relaxation. Beautiful flowers add to the feeling of freshness and the soft tones create a tranquil sanctuary.

On Monday morning, the indoor swimming pool will ease away the throbs of yesterday's champagne breakfast, with tranquil underwater music and a calming atmosphere accentuated by the use of cooling mosaics and bamboo. Large windows look out onto the outdoor patio and allow sunlight to stream through onto the rippling water. Facilities also include jacuzzis, steam and sauna rooms and a WestinWORKOUT Powered by Reebok Gym. Reebok workout machines are installed in two special guestrooms for those who are actively inclined. Alternatively, a running partner can accompany guests who desire a jog along the Bund.

Asia's award-winning Banyan Tree Spa is located within the Westin Hotel and offers the ultimate in pampering for both the body and the soul. After a relaxing massage, return to your room for a further rest in the 'Heavenly Bed' before Shanghai's night draws you back out into town.

There are seven restaurants and bars incorporating Asian, international and Italian cuisine. You can enjoy cigars, cocktails and hot jazz in Niche. For those who've had a good workout in the gym, a glass of fresh fruit juice in the Bliss Bar will re-energize. For food you can decide on anything from al fresco sushi to stone-baked pizza. On Sundays, highly recommended is the 'Westin Brunch', where a feast of free flowing champagne, tantalizing food and live entertainment awaits.

THIS PAGE (FROM TOP): The Crown Deluxe Room with the huge 'Heavenly Bed'; the stunning glass staircase of the hotel's lobby.
OPPOSITE: Lighting the night sky, the Bund Centre's crown guides your way back to the Westin.

FACTS		
ROOMS	331 • service apartments: 113
FOOD	The Stage: international • Prego: Italian • EEST: Chinese, Japanese and Thai • Treats: deli
DRINK	Heavenlies: lounge • Niche: bar • Bliss
FEATURES	Banyan Tree Spa • indoor pool • ballroom and function rooms
NEARBY	the Bund • Huangpu River • Nanjing Road
CONTACT	Bund Centre, 88 Henan Central Road, Shanghai, 200002 • telephone: +86.21.6335 1888 • facsimile: +86.21.6335 2888 • email: rsvns-shanghai@westin.com • website: www.westin.com/shanghai

Shama Luxe at Xintiandi

Having dominated Hong Kong's serviced apartment scene for more than 10 years, Shama, working in partnership with Morgan Stanley, is now opening its doors to visitors and residents in another of Asia's hot cities – Shanghai.

With its growing number of dazzling lights, futuristic skyscrapers, Michelin-star restaurants and designer boutiques, Shanghai is an increasingly buzzing and exciting city.

To complement this thrilling lifestyle, Shama has created 100 luxurious and ultra-glamorous apartments that include Shanghai's most magnificent penthouse suite, which comes with a private rooftop garden and swimming pool.

With its prime location, together with a high standard of personalized customer service and the best quality of amenities, Shama has created its first project in its luxe line—Shama Luxe at Xintiandi. Each apartment is uniquely designed by Italian architect Filippo Gabbiani, whose work includes some of the most magnificent renovations along the Bund. Hardwood flooring, coloured glass walls, retro egg chairs and cubic sofas accentuate the apartments' character. Flat-screen televisions hang on the walls of every room and top-end gadgets

THIS PAGE (FROM TOP): Indulge in luxurious furnishings; each apartment is uniquely designed by Italian architect Filippo Gabbiani.

OPPOSITE (FROM TOP): Meticulous housekeeping service; Shama Luxe's ultra-stylish and magnificent interiors are highly irresistible.

are all part of their meticulous service. The state-of-the-art Health Club offers a full range of unique sporting facilities that can be seen nowhere else in Shanghai.

With its prestigious address at Xintiandi, Shama Luxe is located right in the centre of Shanghai's finest entertainment district with haute cuisine, fashionable drinking holes and designer shops on the nearby cobbled lanes. A multiplex cinema and all the top brands are but a stone's throw away. The apartments are an ideal base for both business and leisure, as Huaihai Road, the Bund and Financial District are only a very short distance by taxi.

To ensure guests make the most of the city, Shama provides a 'no boundaries' membership which fast tracks tenants' social lives. It offers insider advice, plus some irresistible discounts at many top restaurants and retailers, setting them up for both a great night out and a chic night in.

include a DVD player, i-Pod docking and a huge American-style fridge. With accommodations ranging from one-, two- and three-bedroom apartments, all with private balconies, those searching for the ultimate bachelor pad or perfect family home, will find their needs met here.

Shama's attention to detail, however, goes far beyond its looks. Daily cleaning and laundry services, a 24-hour concierge, a fully equipped business centre and café

FACTS		
ROOMS		100 apartments (1, 2, 3 bedrooms)
FEATURES		luxurious, fully-serviced apartments for short-term and long-term stay • high-tech amenities • daily maid service • 24-hours concierge • business centre • indoor pool • spa • gym • mini theatre • indoor tennis court • basketball court • rock climbing • band room with musical instruments • golf driving range • billiard room (snooker and American pool) • karaoke • lifestyle and privilege card • Chinese restaurant • outdoor café • barbeque
NEARBY		Xintiandi • Huaihai Road • the Bund
CONTACT		Block 18, Lakeville Regency, Lane 168, Shun Chang Road, Luwan District, Shanghai, 200021 • telephone: +86.21.6385 1818 • email: info.shanghai@shama.com • website: www.shama.com

PHOTOGRAPHS COURTESY OF SHAMA.

239 Restaurant + Bar

The ultra-modern, stunningly cool interior of 239 Restaurant and Bar is a stark contrast from the busy, colourful street outside. Walking into the bar area—where to one side refined white leather stools stretch the length of an endless smooth white bar and to the other, immaculate brown suede sofas curve around elegant glass tables—a sophisticated urban tone is immediately apparent. Lit panels separate the bar from the main restaurant where dim lighting and dark walls create a stylish dining area.

A simplistic, sleek white sushi bar sits among the dark low-level tables and provides a fun and interactive seating arrangement. Abstract oil paintings, on large square canvasses, are drawn out from the dark moody walls by spotlights. Flickering candles on each table create an atmospheric, romantic ambience and prove useful when looking through the mouth-watering menu. In the background funky, mellow music plays loud enough to add to the sleek, sexy ambience but quiet enough to still enjoy a conversation. The overall effect of the sharp lines, soft lights and the subtle tones and textures is stunning.

239 is a collaboration between locally renowned chef Eduardo Vargas, owner of Azul and Viva, and Ian Robertson, the grand

...a sophisticated urban tone is immediately apparent.

The well-stocked bar continues to stay open well after the kitchen shuts, and you are encouraged to linger longer in the sultry, sophisticated atmosphere, allowing you to extend your chic night out. Post-dinner drinks slip down easily as the dark surroundings flicker in the candlelight and the music gently washes around you.

master behind Face and Sasha's, two hugely successful bars in Shanghai, and as such the service is as smooth as the décor.

The professional bar staff are happy to mix personalized cocktails for you, or if you prefer, beer is served in ice-cold glasses. In addition the staff are very knowledgeable of the extensive wine list. Eduardo works closely alongside executive chef, Eddie Loo, and together the dynamic pair creates exquisite and contemporary food.

The dishes are varied, imaginative yet perfectly simple and range from delicate tasters to hefty main courses. Using only the best ingredients the food is fresh, crisp, succulent, juicy and all dishes explode with flavour. Specialities include the Salmon Ravioli served with Avocado Mousse and Dill Mustard Cream, the Grilled Kobe Strip of Loin Steak with Onion Jam and Tomato Confit, and the exquisitely tender Caramelized Pork Hock with Latté Coffee Sauce.

FACTS

SEATS	100
FOOD	blend of Western, Asian and Tapas
DRINK	extensive wine list • cocktails
FEATURES	ultra-modern setting • restaurant no-smoking
NEARBY	People's Square
CONTACT	239 Shimen Yi Road, near Weihai Road, Shanghai, 200041 • telephone +86.21.6253 2837 • facsimile: +86.21.6253 2837 • email: marketing@239shanghai.com • website: www.239shanghai.com

PHOTOGRAPHS COURTESY OF 239 RESTAURANT + BAR.

Azul + Viva

Nestled within the serene streets of Shanghai's French Concession, Azul + Viva are well-known throughout the city for the fantastic Latino food and the friendly hospitality, not least by the owner himself, Eduardo Vargas, who can be seen frequently chatting to his regulars and checking up on his valued customers.

Sitting atop each other Azul, on the ground floor, is a small funky Tapas Lounge. Its casual atmosphere is reflected both in the design and the eclectic tapas style menu.

Retro wallpaper combines with dark, cushioned fabric walls creating a rich clash of textures and colours. At the back two large, semi-private tables, sunken into the floor and surrounded by vivid cushions, provide a relaxed bed-style dining experience and are ideal for large groups wanting to stretch out and enjoy an evening of Hispanic indulgence and a sangria which comes in four flavours: classic, peach, white and blackberry. Along the other one side, is a startling blue-tiled low bar, ideal for enjoying the wide range of seafood.

Upstairs, Viva offers a more spacious and formal setting decorated with beautiful silk tablecloths and soft candlelit lighting. A glass wall looks out onto the busy yet tiny street below. On another wall, a long wine

THIS PAGE (FROM TOP): *Delectable Latino fare inspires the menu; candlelight and cushioned walls create a casual yet stylish interior.*

OPPOSITE (FROM TOP): *Lush cushions and a sunken floor reflect the 'bed style' dining; artwork, stone and woods imbue a cosy richness to the restaurant's ambience.*

Full of friendly Latino spirit, great food and affordable prices...

cover a whole page of the menu with all kinds of delights and indulgences.

Condé Nast Traveller, in 2004, included Azul + Viva in their list of 66 hot new restaurants worldwide describing it as 'the hottest new kid on the block'. Full of friendly Latino spirit, great food and affordable prices it's still receiving the same attention from the reviewers, and most importantly from its customers.

rack showcases the varied selection of international wines available; the elegant bar provides a perfect spot for tasting them.

The delectable menu for both restaurants is inspired by owner and executive chef, Eduardo Vargas. Originally from Peru he has worked as a chef all over the world including Hawaii, Ibiza and Singapore. His mouth-watering dishes include Peruvian beef tapas, Andalusian baby clams and Ecuadorian mixed seafood ceviche. Renowned for its tasty fare, both locals and foreigners come regularly to enjoy the fried calamari, beef carpaccio, sesame prawns, tempura oysters and crab-fennel wantons. Upstairs you can choose main courses, ranging from Foie Gras with Banana-Lentil Salsa and Tacu-Tacu Cake, to Salmon with Sherry-Honey Glaze, Spicy Tomato Relish and Garlic Mashed Potato. The desserts

FACTS

SEATS	Azul: 100 • Viva: 120
FOOD	Latino fare • tapas-style menu
DRINK	sangria • extensive wine list
FEATURES	sunken tables with 'bed style' eating • sushi bar
NEARBY	French Concession
CONTACT	18 Dong Ping Road, Shanghai, 200031 • telephone: +86.21.6433 1172 • facsimile: +86.21.6433 1173 • email: marketing@azulviva.com • website: www.azulviva.com

PHOTOGRAPHS COURTESY OF AZUL + VIVA.

Bali Laguna

Frequently referred to as one of the most romantic restaurants in Shanghai, Bali Laguna offers an idyllic setting in Jing'An Park. In the centre of the city, moments away from Nanjing West Road and Jing'An Temple, Jing'An Park is an enclosed oasis of lush greenery. The surrounding trees and plants drown out the noise of the busy city outside. Locals come to practice tai chi, wander the winding paths and relax on the small wooden jetty over the pond, watching the bright fish dart beneath the lilies below. In a picturesque Indonesian style house, with an elegant glass frontage, Bali Laguna is built over a tranquil lotus pond at the edge of the park. An outdoor terrace offers shaded al fresco dining amidst a stunning, peaceful atmosphere.

Inside the restaurant, the calming ambience continues with light and natural surroundings. Earthy tones, exposed wood and concrete walls reinforce the tranquillity.

...shaded al fresco dining amidst a stunning, peaceful atmosphere.

Indonesian artefacts decorate the two rooms, light muslin screens separate the tables, an intricate bamboo roof dramatizes, and a long white bar extends along the back of the first floor. Smart waiters wear vibrant sarongs adding a myriad of brightness. The serene background and the simple furnishings convey a sophisticated South-East Asian influence.

The food is authentically Indonesian, specializing in fresh and healthy vegetables and seafood. Traditional spices and herbs, including cumin, coriander, tamarind, lemongrass, ginger and turmeric, are gathered locally and from Indonesia to ensure the dishes are fresh and fiery. You can fill your table with a range of smaller appetizers or choose from a selection of more substantial courses including otak-otak, spicy chilli crab, fried shrimp and vegetable rice, tasty king prawns with lemongrass, traditional rice dish nasi goreng, crisp spring rolls, chicken satay, oxtail soup, grilled fish and beef rendang. The dessert menu includes an enticing range of both Indonesian and Western options including a traditional sweet coconut cake.

The bar serves an extensive range of international wine along with a creative selection of cocktails including the Bali inspired Nusa Dua Sunset. Staying open until 1 am you can relax in the peaceful surroundings after your dinner and enjoy the alluring range of drinks whilst looking out onto the gardens and the restaurant's sparkling reflection in the pond.

FACTS

SEATS	180
FOOD	Indonesian
DRINK	extensive wine list • cocktails
FEATURES	stunning location • pond • lush greenery
NEARBY	Nanjing West Road • Jing'An Temple
CONTACT	Jing'An Park, 189 Huashan Road, Shanghai, 200040 • telephone: +86.21.6248 6970 • facsimile: +86.21.6248 6961 • email: fromedwin@gmail.com • website: www.bali-laguna.com

PHOTOGRAPHS COURTESY OF BALI LAGUNA.

Bar Rouge

On the 7th floor of an impressive neoclassical building nestled into the myriad of architectural styles along the Bund, Bar Rouge has an enviable view across the Huangpu River. Situated on one of the most famous streets in Asia and top 10 attractions in Shanghai it is without doubt well worth a visit. Originally the economic centre of the city, filled with banks and businesses, the Bund is now as much about entertainment as it is hard work; with many other high-end bars and restaurants, it is the ultimate dining area in Shanghai. And Bar Rouge plays a dominant role in this elite location.

Bar Rouge has two distinct personalities: during the day its calm, relaxed atmosphere welcomes people to enjoy an unhurried lunch or an after work drink, but as night time falls it transforms itself into a frenzied, hyper club where the Chinese high-flyers, foreign expats and visitors alike join the ever-lengthening queue to experience some of the best nightlife in Shanghai.

With a stunning, vast terrace, seating 240 people, overlooking the Huangpu River and the impressive buildings of the Oriental Pearl Tower, the Aurora (with the biggest screen in the world), the Jin Mao Tower

...the best nightlife in Shanghai.

Later into the night people flow in for late night drinking and dancing. The staff switch to manic mode with impressive displays of bottle juggling, fire lighting and cocktail shaking. The soft tones from a few hours before are replaced with pumping dance tunes from the international DJs that play regularly here. Guest DJs have so far included José Padilla (Café Del Mar), Claude and Jean Marc Challes (Buddha Bar), and Stephanne Pompougnac (Café Costes).

The menu, created by the Pourcel brothers at Sens and Bund, provides an equally eclectic and varied mix of food. Essentially it is tapas style but based on French cuisine. Specialities include a duo of oyster fresh and fried, and fois gras with smoked eel and apple celery jus.

As a contemporary and international restaurant, a serene and relaxing bar and a late night stylish club, Bar Rouge caters for all tastes and makes full use of its vast terrace and stunning location on the Bund.

THIS PAGE (FROM TOP): The contemporary setting easily switches from laid-back to one of high intensity clubbing.

OPPOSITE: The terrace offers fantastic views of the city; at night, the Bar Rouge terrace is a great place to soak in the party atmosphere.

(housing the highest bar in the world) and the Peace Hotel, Bar Rouge offers an al fresco lunch with the best views in town and is ideal for an early evening drink to watch the sun come down and Shanghai's lights come up. Inside the ambience is calm, with candles, stylish sofas set deep into alcoves, beautiful flowers and mellow beats creating the ultimate place to unwind.

PHOTOGRAPHS COURTESY OF BAR ROUGE.

FACTS

SEATS	360	
FOOD	French	
DRINK	cocktail bar • extensive wine list	
FEATURES	terrace • spectacular views • DJs • open late	
NEARBY	the Bund • Huangpu River	
CONTACT	7th Floor, Bund 18, 18 Zhongshan East Road • Shanghai, 200002 • telephone: +86.21.6339 1199 • facsimile: +86.21.6339 2979 • email: barrouge@volmail.cc • website: www.resto18.com	

Barbarossa

Take a short trip into People's Park and you will find a fairytale castle that rises up out of the trees, glowing enchantingly. A small bridge over the surrounding lake leads you inside to Barbarossa where the orange walls, the vibrant cushions and enticing cocktails welcome you into its relaxed atmosphere.

Bringing a taste of Morocco to Shanghai, Barbarossa's vivacious interior is a magical escape from the urban drone. As the crickets chirp loudly, your only familiarity with the city is the surrounding skyline that's dotted with reminders of its persevering energy and life. Spread over three floors, with numerous Moroccan and Arabian-themed bars, you can enjoy a refreshing drink on the lakeside terrace, submerged in the tranquillity of the park, or a cocktail on the more dramatic rooftop bar where stunning views across the city enhance the magical ambience that the castle exudes. A Bedouin tent, dominated by a four-sided bar, creates a dark and mystical setting whilst next door is a more intimate Arabian bar with floor cushions, candles, rich and colourful silks and low level tables.

The main restaurant is at ground level where the open sides provide a romantic view across the lake. Barbarossa caters for both lunch and dinner and there's a varied choice between international and

THIS PAGE (FROM TOP): Barbarossa's interior offers a completely different world, a true escape from the city; once inside only the imposing skyline reminds you of the surrounding metropolis.
OPPOSITE: The bar upstairs is where you'll find the guest DJs who provide the mellow ambience.

Arabic cuisine. Main courses include the Moroccan-style Prune and Almond Veal, the Tunisian-style Tuna served with Tomatoes and Green Pepper and the delicious Codfish served with a special Lemon Tomato Sauce. If however your main reason for visiting is to experiment with Barbarossa's long list of cocktails and extensive wine list then try the house specials. For example, the fruity Camel's Hump, or the coffee-flavoured Marakesh express. Alternatively the home-made vodka infusions include honey, vanilla, lychee, ginger and wasabi flavours.

To really settle into the serene and calming surroundings traditional shisha pipes are available with a variety of flavours and their presence, bubbling away at intermitting tables, enhances the vibrant Arabian character of Barbarossa.

A resident DJ keeps the upstairs bars energetic with chilled out vibes and the venue is frequently used for various music events. Open until the early hours of the

morning it's easy to get carried away by the background tunes, the slow pace, the warm and vivid interior and the well-stocked bar but even as you leave, crossing the bridge at the end of the night, Barbarossa remains magically enticing.

PHOTOGRAPHS COURTESY OF BARBAROSSA.

FACTS

SEATS	800
FOOD	international and Arabic
DRINK	cocktails • extensive wine list
FEATURES	spectacular views • DJs • shisha pipes
NEARBY	People's Park • Shanghai Art Museum
CONTACT	231 Nanjing Road West, People's Park, Shanghai, 200003 • telephone +86.21.6318 0220 • facsimile: +86.21.6318 0219 • email: jennifer.green@barbarossa.com.cn • website: www.barbarossa.com.cn

Face

A welcoming and tranquil refuge located off Ruijin Road, a street famed in the French Colonial days as 'avenue joffre', Face couldn't be further from its counterparts. Set in the beautiful gardens of the Ruijin Guest House, surrounded by extensive lawns and trees, sits the beautifully restored villa Can Ying Lou. Built in Shanghai's heady pre-war days for a Japanese trader, the building combines the warmth of an old country home with the opulence and wealth of its past.

THIS PAGE (FROM TOP): Traditional artefacts add authenticity and character to the Face; situated in a restored villa, the unique surroundings set this venue apart from the rest.

OPPOSITE (FROM LEFT): Face Bar where an extensive range of drinks are on offer; throughout, there are many opportunities to sit back and soak in the atmosphere.

Either a summer playground or a winter retreat, Face has the rare ability to indulge every mood. As the sun sets in Shanghai's heat, guests can re-live those colonial days with a gin and tonic (a refreshing green tea, a tropical Summer Breeze or even a chocolate mint martini) on the large terrace in front of the house and enjoy the view across the lawn. If the sun is too much then the cool veranda, draped with floating white curtains and bright Asian fabrics provides a more secluded and shaded spot. As the colder weather arrives, head inside and soak up the vibrant décor, relax on the lustrous red sofas or even recline on the luxurious opium bed.

...combines the warmth of an old country home with the opulence and wealth of its past.

The ambience continues inside with a choice of two superb restaurants. Hazara, named after a tribe and region in Afghanistan, offers a tasty selection of Northern Indian cuisine combining healthy rustic with stylishly refined cooking. Its signature dish, Raan e Huzara (Tandoor Shredded Leg of Lamb) is one of many dishes on the menu to come highly recommended across Shanghai. Brimming with exotic antiques and furniture, the restaurant's sensual atmosphere creates a unique dining experience making it a deservedly popular venue for residents and visitors alike.

Equally steeped in character, is Lan Na Thai. Its name 'many rice fields' is an area in northern Thailand and both the food and serene surroundings reflect this. Reputed to be one of the few authentic Thai restaurants in Shanghai, the menu—complete with chef's recommendations—offers all the favourites along with some enticing alternatives. The Green Curry (Gaeng Kiew Wan) and Thai Omelette (Kai Yat Sai) are particularly good. Looking out onto Face's terrace below and the beautiful lawns of Ruijin make Lan Na Thai a perfect setting for both a relaxing lunch and an intimate dinner.

After your meal, return to Face Bar to make the most of the extensive drinks menu. Absorb the peaceful surroundings or even play pool (the pool table blends perfectly into this serene setting. It's made, of course, out of red felt and dark wood to match the rest of the furnishings) before stepping back out onto the bustling streets of Shanghai.

FACTS

SEATS	Lan Na Thai: 80–100 • Hazara: 60–68 • Face: 80–100 outside, 80–100 inside
FOOD	Lan Na Thai: classical Thai cuisine • Hazara: north Indian frontier cuisine
DRINK	extensive cocktail list • wine • single malt selection
FEATURES	beautifully converted colonial house • outdoor terrace • pool table • private dining rooms
NEARBY	French Concession • bars along Maoming Road • Huaihai Road (shopping)
CONTACT	118 Ruijin 2 Road, #4 Building, Ruijin Guest House, Shanghai, 200020 • telephone: +86.21.6466 4328 • facsimile: +86.21.6415 8913

PHOTOGRAPHS COURTESY OF FACE.

Kathleen's 5 Restaurant + Bar

Located on the rooftop of the Shanghai Art Museum in People's Square, Kathleen's 5 is right in the heart of Shanghai. From here it is just a short walk to Nanjing Road and a stroll through the narrow, local streets to the Bund on the river. Just opposite are Shanghai's Grand Theatre and City Hall, situated around People's Square itself. Kathleen's 5 is not only a stunning and sophisticated restaurant but also a convenient one. From the fifth floor you can gaze out at the spectacular views across Renmin Park, People's Square and the surrounding city, providing one of the more impressive views of Shanghai.

The conservatory was built on the roof of the former racecourse clubhouse, and from inside you can benefit from remarkable views of Shanghai's clock tower and beyond. Walking out onto the huge roof terrace you are greeted by an unlimited view of the city. For a light lunch or an afternoon tea it's a great location to sit and observe Shanghai life as it moves through its day below you. From here you can watch the kites flying, the locals waltzing in the square below or gaze out over the Huangpu River across to Pudong. In the summer there's a cooling breeze across the terrace in the evening and the serene and romantic ambience from the restaurant is heightened by the spectacular, dazzling skyline.

Kathleen's 5 is not only a stunning and sophisticated restaurant but also a convenient one.

THIS PAGE (FROM TOP): *The fresh design of the restaurant provides a welcome retreat; outside on the balcony, take in undisturbed panoramic views of the city.*

OPPOSITE: *Right in the middle of People's Square, diners can take in the sights while undercover of Kathleen's 5's conservatory.*

The main dining room features arched columns and the original curved windows, recalling its rich heritage. A perfect retreat in the winter with the warm décor and a stunning 5-m (16-ft) chandelier hanging from the vaulted ceiling, Kathleen's 5's 'Orange Room' creates a sumptuous atmosphere to while away your evening.

The contemporary menu's Mediterranean inspiration reflects Shanghai's international flavour. With speciality dishes like Pan-Fried Black Cod served with Fava Beans and Lobster Butter, Herb-Crusted Beef Tenderloin on a bed of Creamed Spinach, Wild Mushroom Purée and Merlot, the menu is as sophisticated as the restaurant itself.

Kathleen's 5 is owned by American-born restaurateur, author and well-known Shanghai entrepreneur Kathleen Lau. With Kathleen's 5 in Shanghai, she has certainly brought the best of San Francisco dining to the heart of the city.

FACTS

SEATS	restaurant: 350 • garden terrace: 230 • balcony: 120
FOOD	international
DRINK	cocktails • extensive wine list
FEATURES	conservatory and outdoor terrace • spectacular views
NEARBY	People's Park • Nanjing Road (shopping)
CONTACT	5th Floor, Shanghai Art Museum, 325 Nanjing West Road, Shanghai, 200003 • telephone: +86.21.6327 2221 • facsimile: +86.21.6327 0004 • email: info@kathleens5.com • website: www.kathleens5.com

PHOTOGRAPHS COURTESY OF KATHLEEN'S 5 RESTAURANT + BAR.

Lan Kwai Fong, Park 97

Located in a converted 1930s mansion you can find this hedonistic paradise down a quiet, tree-lined lane in the heart of the French Concession, or by strolling through the tranquil pathways of Fuxing Park. But once you've discovered Lan Kwai Fong at Park 97, unlike its peaceful and serene surroundings, you'll soon realize there's nothing quiet about this decadent and bold establishment. Full of fun, energy and high spirits, Park 97 has become an institution in Shanghai for both locals and foreigners.

Encompassing an Italian restaurant, two sophisticated lounge bars and a club, Park 97 caters for a wild night out. Starting off in Baci you can enjoy enticing Italian cuisine such as house-made pasta dishes and legendary thin-thin crust pizzas. A large bar along the front of the restaurant provides prime seating for investigating the liquors and grappa on display. While outside, tables are lined along the edge of the park to make the most of Shanghai's warmer months and the idyllic, al fresco setting.

Sparkling in sophistication and glamour, the recently opened Lux bar bears all the markings of Shanghai's reputation for lavish indulgence with its inky black and glittering gold décor. With its stunning interior, a resident DJ and international guests playing funky house as well as the selection of Italian and Japanese food and enticing selection of cocktails, spirits and champagnes it's certain that Shanghai's latest hotspot will soon evoke worldwide accolades.

THIS PAGE (FROM TOP): KazBar offers a memorable night out; sophisticated Upstairs at Park 97 was voted 'best place to be seen'.

OPPOSITE (FROM TOP): Lux promises to be the hottest new spot in Shanghai; Baci serves delicious Italian cuisine and sprawls out into the gardens of Fuxing Park.

...undoubtedly one of the top venues for a fun night out in Shanghai.

Live music plays regularly with bands from around the globe. On other nights house and guest DJs play their funky house tunes.

With events constantly lined up, from dance parties and fashion shows to carnivals and barbecues, Park 97 turns every opportunity into a vibrant and energetic celebration. Whether it's New Year, Halloween or just another chance to party it's undoubtedly one of the top venues for a fun night out in Shanghai.

California Club, radiating in vibrant red from every surface, is packed from Monday to Sunday with Shanghai's spirited clubbers dedicated to the sounds of the club's resident DJs. Frequent dance parties include the likes of Paul Oakenfold, Norman Jay, Renaissance and Dave Seaman. The music, the people, décor and the cocktails are all equally loud, and combined they create a buzzing, feverish atmosphere.

Upstairs at Park 97 and in the Moroccan-style KazBar Lounge, the red glow continues but the atmosphere mellows. Seductive lighting and a balcony facing the park provide a relaxing space to enjoy drinks from the wine and champagne list.

FACTS		
SEATS	Baci: 140, outside terrace 42 • California Club: 120 • Lux: 120 plus private room for 12 • Upstairs at Park 97: 270	
FOOD	Italian • Western and Japanese snacks	
DRINK	extensive wine list • champagnes • cocktails • liquors	
FEATURES	live music and other regular events • DJs • a whole night out in one venue • outdoor terrace • pool table	
NEARBY	Fuxing Park • French Concession	
CONTACT	2A Gaolan Road, Fuxing Park, Shanghai, 200020 • telephone +86.21.5383 2328 • facsimile: +86.21.6387 4716 • email: park97@lkfgroup.com • website: www.lankwaifong.com	

PHOTOGRAPHS COURTESY OF LAN KWAI FONG, PARK 97.

Mesa Manifesto

In a city famed for high-living, glamour and indulgence, it's reassuring to find a top-quality restaurant focused foremost on its honest, straightforward cooking and great wines rather than the superfluous pretensions that can sometimes be associated with haute cuisine. Although Mesa offers the same exceptionally high standard of food as Shanghai's most elite dining experiences (Australian chef Steve Baker made his name at T8 restaurant), the menu has a simple and down-to-earth approach that makes it a regular favourite with both expats and visitors, as well as with locals.

Formerly an electronics factory, Mesa retains a striking industrial feel with an unusual, eye-catching glass frontage and recycled metal and timber interior. A glassed-in kitchen, stark spiral staircase and split-levels break up the large open space while lush red velvet upholstery glows richly as natural light floods across the restaurant. Upstairs a stunning, south-facing terrace looks out onto the greenery and slower-paced living of the French Concession area where you can relax, soak up the sun and observe the neighbouring activity around the fruit sellers and local shops below.

THIS PAGE: Mesa's ambience emanates from its stylish yet comfortable setting from which guests enjoy the exceptionally high-quality food.

OPPOSITE (FROM LEFT): The kitchen oozes with style as it buzzes away behind its glass casing; adding to the sense of space, the spiral staircase keeps the restaurant open and invites you to enjoy the pleasures of the space upstairs, which includes a large terrace.

At the weekend, Mesa offers undoubtedly one of Shanghai's best home-style brunches with fresh breads and pastries, full fry-ups, eggs benedict, gourmet salads and sandwiches. The friendly service and casual atmosphere make it a popular venue to enjoy a slow morning, reading the papers and watching the city's day progress outside. If you're after a refreshing, al fresco lunch or warming, winter dinner, there's a tasty variety on the menu including fresh, crisp salads, sandwich fillings, locally produced organic vegetables and a variety of seafood and meats. Signature dishes include Carpaccio of Beef with Goat Cheese Gratin, Baked Salmon with Tea-Soba Noodles and Harissa Lamb Pie.

Adjoining the restaurant is Manifesto, a stylish, intimate bar lit by candles and low hanging lanterns. Inviting daybeds align one side creating a luxurious and private hideaway while the dominant three-sided bar inspires a more social setting. The warm and informal atmosphere is ideal for sampling the innovative, delicious cocktails and tasty Western appetizers—including the Baby Burger with Dill, Pickle, Cheddar, Tomato and Mustard and Grilled Chorizo with Sherry—created by Mesa's executive chef Steve Baker. Ideal for an early evening drink and a serene location to linger late into the night Manifesto is the perfect companion to the ever-popular Mesa next door.

PHOTOGRAPHS COURTESY OF MESA MANIFESTO.

FACTS		
SEATS	Restaurant: 130 • Terrace: 50 • Manifesto: 70	
FOOD	Western • seafood	
DRINK	Mesa: extensive wine list • Manifesto: cocktail bar	
FEATURES	terrace • vegetarian options • late night bar	
NEARBY	French Concession • Huaihai Road (shopping)	
CONTACT	748 Julu Road (east of Fumin Road), Shanghai, 200040 • telephone: +86.21.6289 9108 • facsimile: +86.21.6289 9138 • email: info@mesa-manifesto.com • website: www.mesa-manifesto.com	

Sasha's

Located in the centre of the leafy and quiet streets of the former French Concession area sits an impressive, European style, three-storey mansion. It has almost 100 years of revolutionary history and legendary stories and has been occupied by the famous Soong family, government officials, the Japanese Army and a music school before finally emerging in 1998 as Sasha's.

The downstairs bar is inviting and sumptuous with unusual and enormous red lanterns that dominate the soft lighting. The dark wood, long polished bar and fireplace create a colonial ambience heightened by the traditional, grand features of the building

itself. Glass doors open up into possibly the most prestigious and sizeable garden in Shanghai. Surrounded by trees and greenery, the low level lighting and chilled vibes coupled with oversized, sink-into wicker chairs create an idyllic setting for an evening of drinking and it has not gone unnoticed by the rest of the city. In the warmer months the garden is brimming with thirsty customers eager to sample the impressive variety of cocktails, draught beer, premium cognac and fine wine. Bar snacks are available and outside, a stone oven wafts mouth-watering flavours into the night air submitting numerous drinkers to the gorgeous, fresh pizzas.

...possibly the most prestigious and sizeable garden in Shanghai.

The restaurant on the second floor is well known for its delicious steaks; the Kobe Rib Eye will leave you coming back for more. The Pan-Seared Arctic Halibut on Rice with Sautéed Clams is another example from the sophisticated Western menu. Diners can relax and enjoy the fast and friendly service, all the while looking through the original windows out onto the garden below where others take in the evening air over drinks.

For that special occasion, Sasha's third floor lounge is the perfect venue. If you are planning a dinner, the room can seat from 10 to 50 people, or if you are having a party, there is space for up to 150 people.

Whether you have come to Sasha's for a private party, a meal or to relax over drinks in the bar or exquisite gardens, the options ensure the pace of your evening can be as fast or as slow as you choose.

THIS PAGE: The colonial-style restaurant serves modern international cuisine while the vast original windows allow natural light to flood in.

OPPOSITE (FROM TOP): The bar is a great place for a brunch, eggs benedict is a favourite; steeped in history it is a grand setting to sit back and take in the city's night.

FACTS

SEATS	garden: 150 • 1st floor bar: 60 • 2nd floor restaurant: 60 • 3rd floor function room: 10–50
FOOD	modern international • pizza
DRINK	extensive wine list • cocktails • cognacs
FEATURES	converted colonial house • garden terrace • music • pool table
NEARBY	French Concession • Huaihai Road (shopping)
CONTACT	11 Dongping Road, Shanghai, 200021 • telephone: +86.21.6474 6166 • facsimile: +86.21.6474 6170 • email: reservations@sashas-shanghai.com • website: www.sashas-shanghai.com

Sens + Bund

Sens&Bund shares its elite location at 18 Bund with Tan Wai Lou and Bar Rouge and has the same exceptional views of both Shanghai's history along the riverfront and future in the ever-developing skyline.

Jacques and Laurent Pourcel—the youngest chefs to be awarded a prestigious Michelin three star for Le Jardin des Sens in their hometown of Montpellier—visit Sens&Bund at least four times a year to introduce new recipes to the innovative Mediterranean menu. A range of their cookbooks is permanently on display to inspire and tantalize any browsing guest. The rest of the year, executive chef Jerome Largarde, who has worked in both Europe and the US, uses his innovative flair to create some of the best French, Spanish and Italian gourmet food Shanghai has to offer.

The food is sensational, both in taste and presentation. The Pourcel brothers believe every dish should challenge the limit of your senses, of vision, taste, sound, touch and smell and chefs in the glass-lined kitchen do everything they can to achieve this. The delightful smell of fresh baked bread is the

THIS PAGE (FROM TOP): Every detail is carefully considered, from the tableware to the flowers; one of the private rooms offers discrete dining in a sumptuous setting.

OPPOSITE: Guests can enjoy the modern chic ambience inside whilst taking in the spectacular views outside.

...every dish should challenge the limit of your senses...

first of many aromas that indulge you throughout the evening. The appearance of each portion is exceptionally considered and absolutely stunning. Unusual flavours and rich textures are superbly mixed. Specialities include a Lobster Terrine and Duck Breast served with Young Vegetables and Vanilla-flavoured Olive Oil, an Oxtail Consommé with Baby Tomato Ravioli, Roasted Dover Sole Filet with Sweet Corn Purée and Cauliflower Popcorn, and Sautéed Sea Scallops with Rocket Gazpacho and Parmesan Ice Cream.

There are over 300 different wines and champagnes to choose from, each are displayed for your viewing behind the dominant ultra-modern bar that runs along the back of the restaurant.

The room itself, designed by French architect Imaad Rahmouni, has a sophisticated retro feel with a theme of creams and browns that runs throughout. The leather, 1970s-style chairs and booths look comfortable and luxurious while the huge windows, overlooking the river, provide a fresh and natural light, creating an airy and cool ambience by day and a stylish urban chic by night. Two small terraces overlook the Peace Hotel to one side and the Huangpu River on the other. The lights of Shanghai ahead bestow an exquisite and romantic setting in which to savour the many delights that Sens&Bund has to offer.

FACTS

SEATS	165
FOOD	French and Mediterranean
DRINK	wine cellar
FEATURES	Michelin-star chefs • terrace • spectacular views
NEARBY	the Bund • Huangpu River
CONTACT	6th Floor, Bund 18, 18 Zhongshan East Road, Shanghai, 200002 • telephone: +86.21.6323 9898 • facsimile: +86.21.6323 8797 email: sensandbund@volmail.cc • website: www.resto18.com

Simply Thai

Tucked away in a quiet, leafy street in the French Concession, with another restaurant situated in Xintiandi, Simply Thai is no ordinary restaurant. As part of Simply the Group it enjoys the same success as its younger siblings, Simply Life (lifestyle store for beautiful, unique gifts) and the Party People (event management and catering specialists). Unlike other chains, the restaurants have managed to retain a personal feel with friendly service and authentic Thai food.

At one restaurant, a small wooden decked courtyard is shaded by an overhanging tree. With Buddhist carvings, unobtrusive incense drifting from the flower beds, floating lilies in a small pond and soft music drifting in the background, the setting is perfect for al fresco dining.

Inside, the feeling is equally authentic and the dark woods and red upholstery create a welcoming atmosphere for the colder months, or when you simply want to escape from the heat.

The range of signature dishes includes tom yum seafood soup, light Thai fish cakes and a green curry with a perfect blend of chillies, fresh herbs and spices. The extensive menu is changed regularly, however all the favourites, including the spring rolls, have a permanent home here. The drinks list is comprehensive and has an array of cocktails, mocktails, wines and beer on offer.

...the food is wholly authentic and full of flavour.

THIS PAGE (FROM TOP): *The setting is completely relaxed and complements the grand interior; with international acclaim, not least from the Thai Royal family, guests can be confident of the truly authentic Thai cuisine.*
OPPOSITE: *The dark woods and deep red upholstery of the interior create a welcoming atmosphere in all of the Simply Thai restaurants.*

Simply Thai has been voted the best Thai restaurant in Shanghai by magazines such as *That's Shanghai, Shanghai Tatler, Modern Weekly* and *City Weekend*. It sits amongst the 20 most popular restaurants in Shanghai, as stated by *The Zagat Review* and has been reviewed as far a field as the *Sunday Times* in the UK. With such international acclaim, the best recommendation, however, must come from the Thai Royal Family, who frequent Simply Thai on their visits to Shanghai.

With fresh ingredients and fragrant spices flown from Thailand, the food is wholly authentic and full of flavour. The gentle yet attentive service complements the relaxed atmosphere and the lush outdoor courtyard provides a perfect setting to enjoy some of the best Thai food in Shanghai, which is after all fit for a King.

PHOTOGRAPHS COURTESY OF SIMPLY THAI.

FACTS		
SEATS	Xintiandi: 114 • Dongping: 114 • Hongmei: 180	
FOOD	Thai	
DRINK	extensive international wine list • cocktails • mocktails • fresh fruit juices	
FEATURES	outdoor terrace	
NEARBY	French Concession • Xintiandi • Hongmei Road	
CONTACT	corner of Ma Dang and Xing Ye Roads, Shanghai, 200021 • telephone: +86.21.6326 2088 • facsimile: +86.21.6384 6522 5C Dong Ping Road, Shanghai, 200031 • telephone: +86.21.6445 9551 • Lane 3338, 28-29 Hongmei Road, Shanghai, 201103 • telephone: +86.21.6465 8955 • email: enquiry@simplythai-sh.com • website: www.simplythai-sh.com	

T8 Restaurant

Recently voted one of the best 50 restaurants in the world by *Condé Nast Traveller* magazine, T8 must not be missed during your visit to Shanghai. Hidden away down a quiet alley off Xintiandi, a magnet for chic shops, bars and the Shanghai fashionables, the restaurant prides itself on its creative and eclectic mix of modern Australian food.

And so it should. The chef, Australian Stephen Wright, has worked alongside some of the world's culinary heavyweights, including Eric Chavot, and is the honoured recipient of La Chaine de Rottiseaur Commis de Juene, an international award marking excellence in young chefs.

But for all its grandeur the atmosphere is remarkably relaxed and cosy. The interior was created by Spin Design, known for their dazzling work at the Grand Hyatt in Singapore. The soft lighting, rich, dark wood and lacquered furniture throughout the restaurant creates a warm retreat you could happily immerse yourself in, day after day. The snug bar at one end, combined with the comfy bar stools and extensive drinks menu, ensures even those not eating can truly settle into a languidly long

THIS PAGE (FROM TOP): The ambience continues upstairs where the Shanghainese structures blend with contemporary style; the bar is a welcoming spot for those just out for a drink; stylish and modern décor sets the scene for some of the most original dishes in the city.

OPPOSITE: The kitchen is open till late and diners can relax while the chefs create their meals before them.

...a warm retreat you could happily immerse yourself in, day after day.

evening (or afternoon) here. And for those that don't want to miss out on T8's delights, the immaculate open kitchen remains bustling until well after 11.30 pm so there's no hurry to order your meal.

The food itself is equally stylish and contemporary. Essentially modern Australian with an Asian twist, the menu is changed regularly. Choices vary from fusion delights including Beef Carpaccio with Goat Cheese Sorbet to universally adored favourites such as Beef Tenderloin with Onion Marmalade and Red Wine Sauce. Signature dishes include Tataki of Sesame Tuna with Carpaccio of Daikon Radish and Beluga Caviar, and Sichuan High Pie. For the sweet tooth, the chocolate addiction platter consists of chocolate lava cake, silk tart, sorbet, brownie and mousse.

Like the menu, the impressive wine list can also leave you deliberating. The carefully selected wines feature unique labels from around the world and offer a range of boutique wines such as Hill of Grace from Henschke, E&E Black Pepper Shiraz and Pinot Noir Dry River that are rarely found elsewhere in Shanghai.

With one of the city's finest chefs, the tantalizing menu and well over 100 wines to choose from, it's not surprising that T8 is one of the best places to spot celebrities.

FACTS		
	SEATS	90
	FOOD	modern Australian with an Asian twist
	DRINK	extensive wine list • martinis • malt whiskies • cognacs
	FEATURES	comfortable, beautiful surroundings • late kitchen
	NEARBY	Xintiandi
	CONTACT	8 Xintiandi North, Lane 181 Taicang Road, Shanghai, 200021 • telephone: +86.21.6355 8999 • facsimile: +86.21.6311 4999 • email: t8@ghmhotels.com • website: www.ghmhotels.com

PHOTOGRAPHS COURTESY OF T8 RESTAURANT.

Tan Wai Lou

Keeping up with the ever-changing trends of the city, Tan Wai Lou has blended traditional Cantonese cuisine, originally from Guangdong and the southern Yangzi area, with Western influences. The creation is an enticingly eclectic menu with a unique slant and dishes include Special Shrimp Balls with Champagne Sauce, Braised Abalone with Shrimp Seed Sauce, Braised Sea Cucumber and Goose Web in Brown Sauce, Dried Shark's Fin with Crab Meat and assorted Cantonese dim sum alongside a more Western fare including Pan-Fried Fish Fillet in Lemon Sauce, Lamb Chop in Red Wine Sauce and Beef Tenderloin in Thai Red Curry.

Chef Tao Zhihai—recognized as one of the best Cantonese chefs of the moment—oversees the kitchen and regularly changes the menu with new and diverse recipes. Every dish is carefully considered and created using only the freshest organic produce to ensure Tan Wai Lou's meals are as healthy as they are tasty.

Designer Filippo Gabbiani has created a unique and stunning environment. Deep red walls separate the room, evoking a

THIS PAGE: The sashimi bar is adorned with striking red bricks which have been imported from Italy; guests can enjoy fresh fish and an aperitif whilst taking in the stunning views inside and out.

OPPOSITE (FROM LEFT): Views of the other side of the river dominate the windows around the restaurant; private dining is a speciality and guests can have their very own area all to themselves.

...Italian lighting that softens the overall effect, leaving an air of calm sophistication.

sense of privacy at each table. Inset into an alcove in each wall is a unique and beautiful vase shaped lamp giving a sensual glow from the rich, red background. The dark and polished wooden floor is inlaid in parts with exquisite slate and red glass tiles. This impressive and sumptuous surrounding bears the historical character of the building, and of the city itself. And these strong Chinese elements are further complemented by the integration of imported materials and

elegant Italian lighting that softens the overall effect, leaving an air of calm sophistication. Beautiful table linen, designed exclusively for the restaurant, and attentive waiters, dressed in stylish black and red suits, add further elegance.

Nine sophisticated private rooms are adorned with elegant chaise lounges and silk cushions. They can be grouped together for an impressive party or cordoned off for a more private affair. Located on the fifth floor of 18 Bund, Tan Wai Lou shares the same phenomenal views of the Huangpu River as Sens&Bund and Bar Rouge, and the dramatic interior of the restaurant is heightened by its huge windows.

An impressive sashimi bar dominates the back of the restaurant with floor-to-ceiling, red glass bricks imported from Italy and a startling blue bar. From here you can sample the finest fresh fish and enjoy a huge variety of aperitifs whilst looking out onto the spectacular restaurant and the river beyond.

FACTS

SEATS	206
FOOD	Cantonese
DRINK	extensive wine list
FEATURES	sashimi bar • spectacular views • private dining
NEARBY	The Bund • Huangpu River
CONTACT	5th Floor, Bund 18, 18 Zhongshan Dong Road, Shanghai, 200002 • telephone: +86.21.6339 1188 • facsimile: +86.21.6323 8789 email: tanwailou@volmail.cc • website: www.resto18.com

PHOTOGRAPHS COURTESY OF TAN WAI LOU.

Thai Gallery

Stark, sleek and contemporary, Thai Gallery is far from the average Thai restaurant. Rather than re-creating a feel of South-East Asia, by using bright colours and indigenous artefacts, Thai Gallery has taken a minimalist approach with stunning effect.

It's a grand entrance, walking through impressively large doors into the dramatic main restaurant. Austere concrete walls and heavy wooden floors dominate the open space, unusually high ceilings and large windows add spaciousness and light to the minimalist setting and a long white bar looks sleek and smart against the grey slabs behind it. Metallic tables and faintly retro chairs blend into the ultra contemporary surroundings and, along the vast walls, flamboyant and varied pop art brings a powerful brightness to the otherwise stark room. The overall feel of the restaurant is

sleek and sophisticated and even the smart bathrooms are hidden behind an automatic, sliding concrete door. A wide, open staircase leads you upstairs to a more relaxed environment with floor seating and fantastically bright Thai-style cushions.

The paintings vary from pop art Buddhas and abstract portraits to huge orchids, and are all for sale. If you feel inspired to create a masterpiece yourself, crayons sit alongside the salt and pepper grinders on each table and your table-mat doubles conveniently as a canvas.

Unlike the modern décor the food is authentically Thai with rich sauces and tangy zests. Spices and ingredients are bought specially from South-East Asia and combined with locally grown organic produce to create mouth-watering flavours. With over 70 dishes on the menu there is a

THIS PAGE (CLOCKWISE FROM TOP):
Small details show the Thai nature of the restaurant; upstairs the relaxed seating ensures a night of fun; the huge windows cast a comfortable ambience.
OPPOSITE: The open staircase creating a welcome sense of space.

...Thai Gallery has taken a minimalist approach with stunning effect.

temptingly wide selection of the most classic Thai recipes, which includes a delicious Tom Yum Goong (sour and spicy prawn soup with lemongrass), Steamed Mandarin Fish, Larb Gai (minced chicken salad) and the Wok-Fried Crab in a Curry Sauce. For a taste of everything try tod ruom, an assortment of appetizers including prawn cakes, golden pouches, pandan chicken and spring rolls. You can even design your own curry choosing from five essential flavours and adding vegetables, beef or shrimp.

Owner Edwin Ng, who also owns South-East Asian restaurant Bali Laguna, has ambitious plans to keep Thai Gallery one foot into the future, his goal is to make Thai Gallery restaurant the most relaxed and ambient in the city. With background lounge music from superb monthly selections of CDs imported from abroad, enticing cocktails, tatami-style seating and delicious food; it's already well set up for a different yet sophisticated night out.

PHOTOGRAPHS COURTESY OF THAI GALLERY.

FACTS

SEATS	140
FOOD	Thai
DRINK	extensive wine list • cocktails
FEATURES	art for sale • tatami-style seating
NEARBY	Nanjing West Road (shopping)
CONTACT	127 Datian Road by Beijing West Road, Shanghai, 200041 • telephone: +86.21.6217 9797 • facsimile: +86.21.6271 5983 • email: fromedwin@gmail.com • website: www.thaigallery.com.cn

Va Bene

After rambling through the eclectic cobbled lanes of Xintiandi, American coffee shops, French restaurants, restored Shikumen houses and elegant Chinese boutiques you arrive assuredly at the foothills of Tuscany, in the form of Va Bene, Shanghai's most authentic and uniquely styled Italian restaurant.

Following on from the success of the original Va Bene in Hong Kong, a pioneer of the famous Lan Kwai Fong entertainment district, Va Bene Shanghai also benefits from an equally elite location in the heart of the city's most popular shopping and dining area. Va Bene Shanghai also enjoys similar accolades to its thriving Hong Kong sister and within four months of opening was voted the city's best restaurant by a local lifestyle magazine.

A bright cheerfulness envelops you as you walk into the bright, cosmopolitan trattoria. Along the walls are colourful murals of Italian streets. Chandeliers spread a warm light across the wooden floors and bright walls and a conservatory, blossoming with trees, allows natural light to flood in across the restaurant. A private dining room, which seats up to 18 people, is grandly decorated in the style of a rustic Tyrolean Hunting Lodge, complete with animal skins and antlers on the walls. The eccentric atmosphere continues in the lively bathrooms where the walls are, somewhat bizarrely, covered with a butterfly collection.

The authentic Italian menu provides a healthy range of provincial cuisine including home-made pastas and classic Roman-style

THIS PAGE (CLOCKWISE FROM TOP):
Colourful murals of Italian streets adorn the restaurant; the conservatory is a great spot to enjoy the sunshine; Va Bene's wine cellar houses over 100 varieties of wine.

OPPOSITE: The décor stands up to the authentic provincial cuisine evoking a truly Tuscan feel in the heart of Shanghai.

pizzas. Italian chef Alessandro Colombis has gained recognition in restaurants worldwide but his initial inspirations came from his home country and he frequently takes diners on a tour of Italy with authentic flavours from the most popular culinary regions. Try Va Bene's signature dish Linguine Alle Vongole (linguine with clams). As with all the dishes on offer, it combines honest, local cooking with a sophisticated flare. Bread baskets of fresh home-baked grissini and herbed flatbread send mouth-watering aromas around the restaurant. The great selection of wine on offer also comes from various provinces across Italy, and with so many, there is no shortage of choice.

Whether you're basking in the sun streaming through the glass roof or warming up from the cold with a glass of red and a hearty home cooked meal, Va Bene has created a fantastically bright and friendly atmosphere in which you can enjoy some of Shanghai's best Italian cuisine.

FACTS		
SEATS	250	
FOOD	Italian	
DRINK	extensive wine list	
FEATURES	conservatory • distinctive design • fresh pastas and breads	
NEARBY	Xintiandi	
CONTACT	Lane 181 Taicang Road, Xintiandi, Shanghai, 200021 • telephone: +86.21.6311 2211 • facsimile +86.21.5306 6138 • email: vabene@vabeneshanghai.com • website: www.vabeneshanghai.com	

PHOTOGRAPHS COURTESY OF VA BENE.

Yè Shanghai

Yè Shanghai sits comfortably in the trendy Xintiandi complex. Next door to designer boutiques on the distinctive cobbled lanes that are brimming with Shanghai's chic residents, expatriates and visitors alike, this is the perfect location for the contemporary Shanghainese restaurant. Xintiandi houses a combination of traditional 'stone gate' homes of Shanghai, with newly developed buildings tastefully replicated to blend in with their original 1920s neighbours. Yè Shanghai sits within one of these authentically restored shikumen houses.

Inside, the décor is truly stunning with immaculate dark polished wooden floors, beautiful wooden beams and wooden pillars which stretch up past the mezzanine level to the astonishing and exposed original slate roof. Guests can choose to sit at the well-spaced tables—clean and elegantly laid with crisp white linen tablecloths—or at

the more sumptuous teahouse booths, scattered with velvet and silk cushions, which are situated around the edge of the restaurant. Sitting upstairs you can marvel at the beautiful architecture and opulent surroundings whilst downstairs you can soak up the rich atmosphere and warmth in the dark wooden booths, that are lit by overhanging Chinese lamps, and look out over the bustling streets.

The restaurant was designed by New York architect Tony Chi who has captured and preserved all of the original features of the shikumen home whilst adding his own modern touches. One example is the use of a mezzanine level to enhance the sense of space and light. The design is such that as you enter there's an overall sense of luxurious old-style grandeur immediately softened by the tasteful and fresh simplicity of the white walls and tables.

THIS PAGE (CLOCKWISE FROM TOP): The unique décor of the restaurant draws from the best of old Shanghai with a modern twist; the menu features traditional Shanghainese as well as dishes from Jiangsu and Zhejiang; the choice of tables extends from ground level to mezzanine, from private booth to open space.

OPPOSITE: The location, right in the heart of Xintiandi, provides a truly authentic setting for Yè Shanghai. In an old renovated shikumen house, it is unmistakably Shanghai chic.

...luxurious old-style grandeur immediately softenend by tasteful and fresh simplicity...

Some aspects of the menu are traditionally Shanghainese such as the Drunken Prawns and Smoked Pomfret. And there are also the signature dishes of Sea Cucumber with Mild Chilli Sauce and Deep-Fried Whole Prawn with a Broad Bean Sauce. There is also an alluring choice of modern interpretations of Jiangsu and Zhejiang cuisine and wonderfully fresh seafood including Mushroom in a Crispy Tofu Skin, Shredded Mandarin with Vegetables and a veritable feast of both meat and vegetable dumplings.

Yè Shanghai is part of Elite Concepts family of restaurants and bars—including Zin Wine Bar & Grill—that are located across Asia. They're owned by a Hong Kong enterprise which has future plans for a worldwide expansion. This is good news for food lovers who may be able to enjoy Yè Shanghai's unique adaptations of Shanghai cuisine all over the world; from Tokyo to London, Paris and New York.

PHOTOGRAPHS COURTESY OF YÈ SHANGHAI.

FACTS

SEATS	157 (including 4 VIP rooms)
FOOD	modern Shanghainese
DRINK	extensive wine list
FEATURES	restored shikumen house
NEARBY	Xintiandi
CONTACT	388 Huang Pi Nan Road, Xintiandi, Shanghai, 200021 • telephone: +86.21.6311 2323 • facsimile: +86.21.6311 3311 • email: yss@elite-concepts.com • website: www.elite-concepts.com

ZIN wine bar + grill

Zin is located in a charming and historic 1920s Shikumen building that sits on the edge of Yangzhong Park. This landmark building was once the offices of *China Youth*, the Chinese Communist Party's first magazine, which published the early works of a young Mao Zedong along with the first Marxist-Leninist tracts.

An oasis in the midst of downtown Shanghai, the restaurant is surrounded by the park's greenery. A tranquil patio garden situated at the rear of the restaurant features a delightful bubbling stream that runs past, drowning out the surrounding traffic. From here, guests have the rare pleasure of enjoying both the verdant scenery and the futuristic architecture of Shanghai's skyline.

A wine bar and grill serving delicious wine country cuisine, Zin is named after the

THIS PAGE (FROM TOP): The glass-walled wine cellar houses more than 200 different wines; the view of the night skyline through the wine bar atrium makes for a stunning backdrop.

OPPOSITE (FROM LEFT): As well as the popular wood-fired pizzas, Zin's menu offers an array of wine country cuisine; guests can sit on the patio terrace where the sound of a running stream replaces the usual bustle of the city streets.

Zinfandel wine grape and features a glass-enclosed wine cellar that showcases the restaurant's impressive selection of wines from all over the world.

The first floor dining room displays a contemporary interior that retains the original historic architecture with exposed brickwork, wooden roof beams and whitewashed walls. From the open kitchen, the tantalizing aroma of stone-baked pizzas fills the room. The innovative menu features cuisine from the wine countries around the world. In addition to the Wolfgang Puck-style pizzas there are grilled steaks, deliciously fresh pastas and vibrant healthy salads. Other popular menu items include the Seared Foie Gras, Veal with Rosemary Polenta, and Saffron and Wild Lamb Gremolata.

As you would expect, food and wine go hand-in-hand at Zin and the friendly staff are always happy to offer advice on which wine to pair with which dish.

The second floor, which overlooks the park, houses the spacious wine bar, where there are over 200 different wines available for tasting. To accompany your glass of wine, there is a menu of tasty 'small bites'.

Whether it is to sip Zinfandel in the cosy wine bar upstairs or to dine in the restaurant downstairs, this stylish yet casual spot allows guests to enjoy the Shanghai skyline in completely tranquil surroundings and settle into a relaxed evening of great food and great wine.

FACTS		
SEATS	restaurant: 112 • wine bar: 100
FOOD	wine country cuisine
DRINK	wine cellar • cocktails
FEATURES	restored Shikumen house • outside terrace • rooftop balcony
NEARBY	Yangzhong Park • Xintiandi
CONTACT	Number 2 Lane 66 Dan Shui Road, Shanghai, 200020 • telephone: +86.21.6385 8123 • facsimile: +86.21.6385 1312 • email: zin@elite-concepts.com • website: www.elite-concepts.com

PHOTOGRAPHS COURTESY OF ZIN WINE BAR + GRILL.

Annabel Lee Shanghai

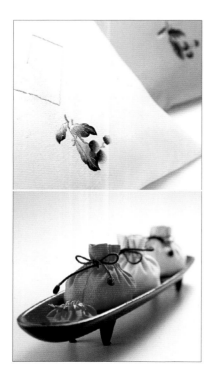

Specializing predominantly in beautiful Chinese silks, Annabel Lee Shanghai offers a range of elegant gifts and accessories for the home. Ranging from sumptuous silk pyjamas to exquisite notebooks there is a wonderful variety on display. Sharing an exceptional quality and individual handmade touches, each product is a delight to look at, making Annabel Lee a perfect place to search for that really special gift.

The team of designers working at Annabel Lee have a recognizable interest in the heritage and traditional culture of China.

Using the highest quality silk from the most famous regions of China, which include Shanghai itself, Suzhou, Hangzhou and Shandong, Annabel Lee applies traditional silk embroidery to create stunning finishes to each design. Produced mainly in the Jiangsu, Guangdong, Hunan and Sichuan provinces, the legend of silk embroidery derived thousands of years ago when sewing was common in most households. The traditions and techniques were passed from generation to generation from mother to daughter. Using thread several times thinner

THIS PAGE (FROM TOP): Cushions, bags, purses and much more are available in sumptuous silks and beautiful embroidery.

OPPOSITE (FROM TOP): The sheer variety of products on offer makes Annabel Lee a superb place for gifts; the shop is laid out in such a way that browsing is a completely relaxing experience.

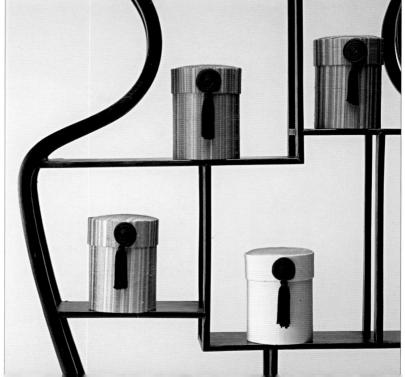

ft) flagship store in 2006, guaranteeing that Annabel Lee accessories are easily found all over the city. It offers a range of products through some of Shanghai's most prestigious hotels—including the Portman Ritz-Carlton and Four Seasons Shanghai.

The overtly friendly service and fresh, simple layout within the shop creates a laidback and welcoming environment in which to browse. The products themselves combine an interesting and visually stunning variation that blends luxurious and traditional materials with highly contemporary designs. Whilst the designers continue to gain inspiration from China's past they are certainly at the forefront of Shanghai's future with a striking range of highly fashionable gifts and accessories.

than a strand of hair and hundreds of different colours, the result is astonishing. The influence of Western culture at the beginning of the 19th century and the prolonged wars and social turbulence, threatened this time-honoured method of embroidery. However, it managed to survive the political upheavals and Annabel Lee now continues to implement it into the modern culture of Shanghai.

Annabel Lee first opened in 2001, it now has a shop in the popular area of Xintiandi where it sits comfortably alongside well-known heavyweight brands such as Shanghai Tang. It also opened its 300-sq-m (3,229-sq-

FACTS	PRODUCTS	bags • home accessories • silk cushions • jewellery boxes • cushion covers • bedlinen • gifts • cases
	FEATURES	silk • hand-made embroidery
	NEARBY	flagship store near the Bund • store in Xintiandi
	CONTACT	Bund flagship store: No. 1, Lane 8, Zhong Shan Dong Yi Lu, the Bund, Shanghai, 200002 • telephone: +86.21.6445 8218 • facsimile: +86.21.6323 0093 • Xintiandi store: Unit 3, House 3, North Block, Xintiandi, Lane 181, Taicang Road, Xintiandi, Shanghai, 200021 • telephone and facsimile: +86.21.6320 0045 • email: info@annabel-lee.com • website: www.annabel-lee.com

PHOTOGRAPHS COURTESY OF ANNABEL LEE SHANGHAI.

Annly's Antique

Located over 5,000 sq m (53,820 sq ft) in the Qibao district of Shanghai, Annly's Antique is made up of three vast warehouses: Tea & Treasure, Gallery and Inventory Room. They are all centred around a pristine courtyard with potted trees and flowers, antique wooden carts and striking statues. At first glance it's clear the buildings and courtyard have been meticulously cared for. Looking closer at the antiques themselves, you will find the same attention to detail and quality in the restoration. The showrooms are huge and magnificent with a second floor gallery, impressive staircases, wooden floors and warm lighting. They are filled with all kinds of antique furniture and accessories from the mainstream to the bizarre.

All delicately restored, you can find old typewriters, pianos, clocks, lamps, old-style coffee makers, ice boxes, as well as a wall of carpenter's tools. Antiques discovered and brought back from provinces across China scatter the the Tea & Treasure Room, such as Tibetan chests, Mongolian boxes, Shanxi cabinets, Zhejiang canopy beds, Shandong lady's chests and interesting sculptures of different sizes.

On the mezzanine level of the Gallery, contemporary paintings, from local Chinese artists, are displayed on the walls above the ornate furniture. Friendly staff are enthusiastic and happy to show you around the dramatic showrooms and share valuable in-depth knowledge and stories behind each of the antiques. You are also welcome to wander around the impressive rooms at your own pace. The Inventory Room is filled with furniture still awaiting much needed loving care and attention. Staff welcome you to browse through the rows and rows of antiquated chests, chairs and cabinets as they wait in line for restoration.

After taking in the enormous showrooms you can relax in a snug tearoom and enjoy local Chinese tea whilst experiencing a traditional tea ceremony. You can learn the fascinating history and culture behind many of the teas available, which include green tea, chrysanthemum and pu-er tea, as well as details on the production, brewing and drinking of Chinese tea. With its stunning setting and vast selection of antiques, it's easy to spend a whole afternoon wandering through the beautiful showrooms and browsing these items from the past.

Your shopping experience at Annly's Antique is one you will treasure, and the staff's eagerness to enlighten you as best they can, ensures it is an interesting one.

THIS PAGE: The bright, wide open spaces of the Gallery and its wooden floor lend a homely ambience.

OPPOSITE: From the open courtyard to the vast warehouses, you'll find sculptures, paintings, exquisite furniture and antiques.

PHOTOGRAPHS COURTESY OF ANNLY'S ANTIQUE.

FACTS

PRODUCTS antique furniture and accessories • sculptures • paintings
FEATURES beautiful showrooms • tearoom
NEARBY Hongqiao
CONTACT No 68, Lane 7611 Zhongchun Road, Shanghai, 201101 • telephone: +86.21.6406 0242 • facsimile: +86.21.6405 7322 • email: anntique@online.sh.cn • website: www.annlychyn.com

Bund 18

THIS PAGE: *The building and its original features were painstakingly restored by a team of Venetian architects from Kokaistudios. The result is a Bund 18 from its heydays.*

OPPOSITE (FROM TOP): *Luxury brands are a part of Bund 18, offering Shanghai's shoppers the best from around the world; the vast atrium forms the core of the building and features grand décor.*

At the beginning of the 20th century, the Bund was the centre for colonial shipping, banking and trading in China. Forming the main street of what was then the British concession it was the hub of the city. For decades however, many of the buildings on the Bund were left empty and neglected. With businesses once again dominating the historic waterfront, Bund 18 is one of a few initiatives that has introduced shopping and entertainment into the area and is a huge contributor to the Bund's reputation for

housing some of the most elite retail boutiques, restaurants and bars in Shanghai.

Formerly China's headquarters to the Chartered Bank of India, Australia and China, Bund 18 was built in 1923. Its dramatic, column fronted style was originally designed by British architects Palmer and Turner. A painstaking two-year renovation project, finished by a team of Venetian architects from Kokaistudios, has brought the neoclassical building back to its former glory retaining all its original features. It now boasts luxury brand retailers, Michelin star restaurants and some of the city's most spectacular nightlife with unprecedented views of the Huangpu River and the futuristic skyscrapers of Pudong.

At street level and on a second mezzanine floor, Bund 18 houses a sophisticated group of luxury brand clothing, accessory and jewellery retailers and a café. The list includes Cartier, Zegna,

...the neoclassical building back to its former glory...

Boucheron, Patek Philippe, Aquascutum, Emperor Watch and Jewellery, Gabbiani Glass, YOUNIK, Ports 1961, Bree and Sibilla Café. Set around a 7-m (23-ft)-high atrium with striking columns and mosaic marble floor, it's the ultimate designer boutique mall and Shanghai's shoppers flock here to pick up the latest luxury items. Most notably, YOUNIK is Bund 18's concept store showcasing a select group of talented young designers from China, and features fashion, jewellery and accessories.

The Creative Centre on the 4th floor is a multi-functional event and exhibition venue. Here, the charm of old Shanghai mixes with the roaring energy of the new, and adds individuality and glamour to any occasion.

With Tan Wai Lou on the 5th floor, Sens&Bund on the 6th and Bar Rouge on the 7th, Bund 18 is home to some of Shanghai's best nightlife. Indeed, standing proudly on the Bund, this shopping and lifestyle haven reflects the city it belongs to. It is fully revived and once again at the heart of things.

PHOTOGRAPHS COURTESY OF BUND 18.

FACTS		
RETAILERS	Cartier • Zegna • Boucheron • Patek Philippe • Aquascutum • Emperor Watch and Jewellery • Gabbiani Glass • YOUNIK • Ports 1961 • Bree
FOOD	Bar Rouge: French • Tan Wai Lou: Chinese • Sens&Bund: French • Sibilla Café: Italian
DRINK	Bar Rouge • Sibilla Café
FEATURES	renovated building • elite brands • elite restaurants
NEARBY	the Bund • Peace Hotel
CONTACT	Bund 18, 18 Zhongshan East Road, Shanghai, 200002 • telephone: +86.21.6323 7066 • facsimile: +86.21.6323 7060 • email: info@bund18.com • website: www.bund18.com

Hong Merchant

In a beautifully renovated longtang house down a quiet lane in the heart of Shanghai's French Concession you'll find Hong Merchant, a stunningly original antiques shop. The house, built in the 1930s, once belonged to a French officer and is an appropriate setting for this Chinese-French-inspired gallery. Restored by Hong Merchant itself the house retains all the original features with beautiful, trodden, wooden floors, exposed brick walls revealing the seal of the company that made them and bright, spacious rooms with high ceilings and vast lead-glass windows. The upstairs balcony and downstairs sun room look out onto a lush garden.

Lining the corridors, dominating the marble reception and blending flawlessly into rooms throughout the two-floored house, are pieces of immaculately restored Chinese

THIS PAGE (FROM TOP): Bright spacious rooms and wooden floors add decadence to this beautifully restored house; you are encouraged to feel the textures and contours of the objects and antiques.

OPPOSITE (FROM TOP): Celebrated painters' works adorn the pastel coloured walls; the cosy sun room opens out onto the vast garden.

...you'll find Hong Merchant, a stunningly original antiques shop.

They apply an enthusiastic and dedicated eye to discovering and restoring some of the country's finest antiques that are steeped in Chinese history and heritage.

Hong Merchant also promotes local artists and hanging on the walls are works of various celebrated painters. When passing through, artists will often stay in this bohemian mansion, so as you wander through the rooms admiring the art and antiques, keep your eye out for a future Picasso.

furniture. Elegant bronzes, statues and contemporary works of art restore the house to its former glory creating a stunning environment to browse through Hong Merchant's exceptional collection. Unlike a museum you are encouraged to feel the textures and study the detailed workmanship on each of the restored pieces. Peering into each room you catch a glimpse of life in an early-20th-century Shanghai home.

Each room has its own individual character and the furniture is displayed to reflect it. Downstairs, at the back of the house, a snug room with exposed brick walls is warmed by beautiful red lacquers and woods creating a homely and rich cosiness. Upstairs, looking out onto the balcony from the green room, dark furniture and rustic colours inspire a calm and serene atmosphere. By creating a home for the furniture and paintings, customers are able to visualize each piece in their own homes.

Together, the team behind Hong Merchant has many years of experience in archaeology, design, the study of Chinese culture and antique furniture collecting.

FACTS

PRODUCTS antique furniture • modern-day designs • paintings
FEATURES natural display of furniture • beautifully restored longtang house
NEARBY French Concession
CONTACT by appointment, Number 3 Lane 372 Xing Guo Road, Shanghai, 200052 • telephone: +86.21.6283 2696 • facsimile: +86.21.6283 9721 • email: jpweber@uninet.cn, an-cecil@online.sh.cn • website: www.hongmerchant.com

PHOTOGRAPHS COURTESY OF ART KOOIJ + LIU SHENGHUI.

Hu + Hu

Social, insightful, thoroughly satisfying and dangerously tempting, this vast warehouse housing hundreds of pieces of antique Chinese furniture is the ultimate shopping experience. Sisters-in-law, Lin and Marybelle Hu, opened their showroom and warehouse in 1998. Since then Hu and Hu has become synonymous with quality and beauty. With 20 years experience of collecting and restoring antiques, Lin has a gifted eye when scouring for the most interesting furniture and antiques and restoring them to their former splendour. Marybelle is equally skilled with a degree in Art History and years of working at Taipei's National Palace Museum and at Sotheby's.

Spread over a 1,500-sq-m (16,145-sq-ft) warehouse and spilling onto the yard in front, Hu and Hu offers an abundance of Chinese heritage and culture through its goods, which range diversely from intricately detailed, miniature boxes to huge Chinese wardrobes. There are sculptures, Tibetan chests, wedding beds, cabinets,

THIS PAGE (FROM TOP): Antiques from across China are brought here to be carefully restored; a stunning Chinese day bed—for information on shipping just ask the staff, it's all part of the great service.

OPPOSITE: All items are skillfully restored to their original state; shoppers are welcome to browse along the rows and rows of antiques.

chairs, tables, mirrors, cases, stools, wooden carvings, candlesticks, desks and anything you can't see you can have custom-made. The two warehouses display carefully laid out antiques, recently bought in from across the country. Some pieces are awaiting restoration and they can be renovated to your very own specifictions. (China has regulations for exporting antiques so ask for details before you buy). You can also specially order replicas of an item you have seen before which will be delivered directly to you. It's all part of the service at Hu and Hu. Whether restored antiques or modern day furniture, every piece is guaranteed to be of exceptional quality and even out-of-sight details, the bottom of the drawer, the back of the cupboard, have been meticulously and lovingly restored or made.

Personal service is as important here as the antiques themselves and guests receive the same meticulous attention as the restored furniture. Always close by, there's never a shortage of friendly staff to help, advise and inform, whether it's the history of Tibetan chests or the best way to export a seven-foot Chinese bed. There are refreshing beers and cooling tea on offer while you browse through the huge array of furniture.

With so many beautiful antiques bought in from regions across China, from deep in the mountains of Tibet to the capital of Beijing, Hu and Hu is as much an insight into China's history as a unique and wonderful shopping experience.

FACTS

PRODUCTS	antique furniture • custom-made furniture • gifts • accessories
FEATURES	restoration • shipping
NEARBY	Gubei • Hongqiao Airport
CONTACT	Cao Bao Road, Alley 1885, #8, Shanghai, 201101 • telephone: +86.21.3431 1212 • facsimile: +86.21.5486 2160 • email: hu-hu@online.sh.cn • website: www.hu-hu.com

PHOTOGRAPHS COURTESY OF HU + HU.

Jooi Design

Jooi Design arrived on the Shanghai fashion scene in 2002. Founded in 1999 in Hong Kong, Jooi Design is owned and run by Trine Targett and Gitte Nielsen, and is a Danish design company specializing in fashion accessories and lifestyle products.

The studio shop and showroom can be found in an old candy factory, now called the International Arts Factory, on Lane 210 off Taikang Road, which is more affectionately recognized as Art Street. This Soho-esque corner of Shanghai has attracted many designers and artists creating a Bohemian community, complete with cafés, shops and galleries, and has transformed this sleepy lane reprieved from demolition, into a haven for creative souls.

A startling fresh and bright space, on the second floor of the stark, dimly lit building filled with art studios and other design outlets, Jooi Design's showroom portrays the simple elegance that can be seen in all of Targett and Nielsen's designs. Their collection includes fashionable bags, scarves, pillows, blankets, gift accessories, notebooks and photo albums and the company has plans to introduce a one-of-a-kind limited edition clothing line.

THIS PAGE (FROM TOP): Scarves and bags are just a tiny part of the selection at Jooi Design; the shop's layout and ambience is a welcome environment.

OPPOSITE (FROM LEFT): Part of the Voyage leather collection, this bag is just one example of Jooi's impeccable style; on display at Jooi, simple elegance is evident throughout.

...the sophisticated products are guaranteed to be fashionable for many years to come.

Everything is made to pristine quality; bags ranging from simple everyday handbags to glamorous evening bags, all have unique and delightful finishing touches, their notebooks are beautifully bound in coloured leathers and the stunning silk cushions on display complete the elegance and softness that fills the room.

The product lines are continuously updated and include 'Oriental Expression' which combines 1920's bourgeois lifestyle in Shanghai with modern chic, and the 'Urban Comfort' line which incorporates a softer, more sensual style. There's the select range of Jooi Design Classics for which the company is famed for. The Butterfly Pavilion bag is a favourite, and combines both Asian and Western influences with vibrant fabrics and handles inspired by the pavilion rooftops in the Chinese gardens. These bags are permanently available at the store.

Jooi Design items are familiar across Shanghai and can be bought from various retailers around the city. They also command recognition on a more worldwide level with designs selling in the V & A Museum and Harrods in London, Le Bon Marché in Paris and Frydendahl in Copenhagen.

Combining both a local and Western sense of style, Jooi Design appeals to an international market and, while its designs continue to develop and evolve, the sophisticated products are guaranteed to be fashionable for many years to come.

PHOTOGRAPHS COURTESY OF JOOI DESIGN.

FACTS

PRODUCTS	handbags • scarves • clothing • blankets • cushions • gift accessories
FEATURES	modern and unique designs
NEARBY	shops • cafés • bars • art galleries on Taikang Road • French Concession
CONTACT	2nd Floor International Artist Factory, Taikang Road Lane 210, Shanghai, 200025 • telephone: +86.21.6473 6193 • facsimile: +86.21.6415 2386 • email: studio@jooi.com • website: www.jooi.com

Number D Gallery

Artist and designer Jiang Qiong Er opened Number D Gallery in June 2004. Growing up in a family of artists and creators—her grandfather was an admired Chinese painter and her father, Xing Tonglie, an architect who designed the Shanghai Museum—she has been surrounded by artistic influences throughout her life. Having studied in Paris, she now spends her time between Shanghai and France and this assimilation of East and West is clearly seen in her designs. Regularly profiled in *Elle*, and many other magazines, Jiang is becoming an increasingly familiar face both in and out of the fashion circles in Shanghai and Paris.

Keeping up with the fast-paced developments of Shanghai, she has created a unique and dramatic gallery exhibiting bold and abstract paintings, striking furniture that's both practical and conceptual, beautiful Chinese-influenced jewellery and a dazzling collection of sculptures, vases and varying objects of every shape and size.

The 1,000-sq-m (10,765-sq-ft) gallery is finished in an equally vibrant and differing array of materials. With

THIS PAGE (FROM TOP): Good use of fabrics and furniture divide the unique gallery; bold designs dominate the vast space at Number D Gallery.

OPPOSITE (FROM LEFT): Texture is important to artist, Jiang. Her paintings are rich in texture and their display, alongside traditional Chinese furniture, shows the scope of the gallery.

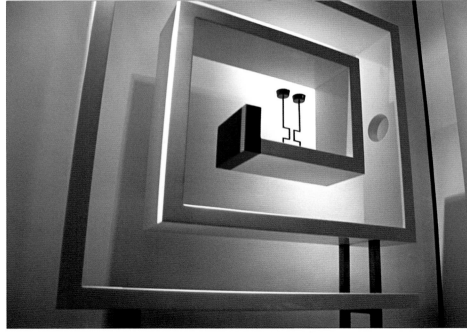

its metal doors and stairs, coloured pipes, multi-level exhibitions and red screens, it's a visual feast. The grey floors, red walls and Chinese lamps enhance the warmth of the Chinese furniture immaculately displayed while in other areas full-length windows and stark lighting have an impressive effect on the sleek, futuristic tables and chairs.

The elegant jewellery is similar in its contemporary and original design, yet there is a clear Chinese influence with rich reds, golds and Chinese symbols artistically adapted. The paintings and photographs also share this dynamic approach to design and are rich with texture.

There's also a salon de thé—library and a projection room—to further indulge your senses. With vases, pots and sculptures of all possible shapes filling fantastically designed shelves throughout the gallery, it's difficult to keep focused on one object.

The gallery is situated in Suzhou Creek and the environment surrounding it reflects the dynamic designs within. Historically the industrial centre of the city, the old factories are now giving themselves up to art studios and galleries, creating a new generation of Shanghai artists and a new era for Suzhou Creek. However, it is the huge variety of furniture, jewellery, sculptures, paintings and photographs in such a fresh and inspiring space that ensures Number D Gallery's unique position amongst the many other galleries it sits beside.

PHOTOGRAPHS COURTESY OF NUMBER D GALLERY.

FACTS

PRODUCTS	paintings • photographs • furniture • sculptures • jewellery
FEATURES	gallery • salon de thé • library • projection room
NEARBY	Suzhou Creek
CONTACT	2nd Floor, Building 15, 1518 Xikang Road, Shanghai, 200060 • telephone: +86.21.6226 2109 • facsimile: +86.21.6299 4289 • email: info@numberD.com • website: www.numberD.com

Shanghai Tang

osmopolitan, confident and brimming with class, Shanghai Tang is China's world-class luxury brand. Using vibrant and bold colours, exquisite and radical designs and sporting a highly desirable brand label, it has become the epitome of China chic.

Even in its early beginnings in 1994, as a small tailoring boutique in Hong Kong, Shanghai Tang managed to attract over 1 million visitors within its first year. Now, with an international network of 19 boutiques around the world—in London, Paris, New York, Tokyo, Hong Kong and Singapore—visitors will be soaring into tens of millions.

Fittingly, there are three outlets dotted around Shanghai; two in Puxi, one in Pudong. With a rich past of exoticism and excess, Shanghai, the 'Paris of the Orient', is now at the forefront of international fascination and has managed to attract all the luxury brands which are intent on

discovering this huge new market. With its fusion of 'East-meets-West' and a strong identity of cosmopolitan extravagance, it's easy to understand why Shanghai Tang has become a leader in this game.

Branching out into home furnishings and gifts, Shanghai Tang sells a range of interesting and unexpected goods. Alongside its range of clothing and accessories, pepperpots, teapots, umbrellas, dressing gowns, bedlinen, cushions and towels all bear the bold characteristics of Shanghai Tang and are emblazoned with the distinctive logo. You can even buy a travel pack complete with eye mask, slippers and pillow all made from the finest silk. It is, however, the line of clothing that garners such respect and adoration from its many fans. Indeed, it's difficult to find another store filled with such intense, brilliant and bold designs. With silk jackets in shocking pink

THIS PAGE: From cushions to tableware, clothing to perfume, all in a quintessentially Shanghainese style.

OPPOSITE (FROM TOP): The dressing gown from the Forbidden City collection; exuberant colours and exceptional quality of Shanghai Tang.

It's difficult to find another store filled with such intense, brilliant and bold designs.

spring collection was inspired by Jing Xi (Peking Opera), where the extravagant and rich costumes seen on stage provided the basis for a more practical yet equally exuberant design. Its daring vision and à la mode style however brings it totally up to date and if you want to be authentically 'Shanghai Chic', you will need at least one garment from Shanghai Tang in your wardrobe.

and stunning dresses in oranges and luminous greens, the Shanghai Tang shopping experience arouses the strongest visual reactions. And if any shop might encourage you to 'blow it on your credit card', this is without doubt the one.

Traditional Chinese culture inspires most of the Shanghai Tang designs. A recent

FACTS

PRODUCTS	clothing • accessories
FEATURES	dynamic and vibrant designs
NEARBY	various hotels • Xintiandi
CONTACT	Jinjiang Hotel, Shop E, 59 Maoming South Road, Shanghai, 200020 • telephone +86.21.5466 3006 • facsimile: +86.21.5466 3011 Shangri-La Hotel, Lobby Level, 33 Fu Cheng Road, Pudong, Shanghai, 200120 • telephone: +86.21.5877 6632 • facsimile: +86.21.5877 6635 Xintiandi Plaza, 15 Xintiandi North Block, 181 Taicang Road, Shanghai, 20002 • telephone: +86.21.6384 1601 • facsimile: +86.21.6384 4106 • email: contactus@shanghaitang.com • website: www.shanghaitang.com

PHOTOGRAPHS COURTESY OF SHANGHAI TANG.

Shanghai Trio

In 1998 Virginie Fournier arrived in Shanghai from France. Walking around the streets she was inspired by the colours, the frenetic pace, the vibrancy of the city and even the quilts and washing hanging out to dry down almost every alleyway. With a huge interest and respect for China's true way of life she joined up with two other European friends living in Shanghai and set out to discover more about local Chinese craftsmen and the wealth of Chinese fabrics. They travelled around the countryside, slowly gathering artefacts from different provinces and returned each time with new inspiration and ideas. In December the same year Shanghai Trio was born and its first collection was displayed in a café in Shanghai—the products were all sold within two hours. Initially using hotels, galleries and boutique shops to distribute their goods, Shanghai Trio now has its own boutique

shop, situated in the fashionable area of Xintiandi and a showroom in a beautifully renovated house on Fuxing Road in the leafy and shaded French Concession area.

Shanghai Trio creations include creative bags, beautiful bedlinen, fabric shoes, scarves, shawls and even mobile phone holders all made from the best Chinese fabrics and varying in colours from rosehip pink to vibrant turquoise. Searching Mongolia, Xinjiang, Jiangsu, Zhejiang and provinces across China for the best cashmere, wool, linen and cotton, the range of textures and colours that make up Shanghai Trio's designs is astounding. Much of the material used is steeped in history and tradition—including the mud silk from South China. Every item is handmade in the

THIS PAGE: The fabrics at Shanghai Trio are sourced from all over China and only the best are used in the workshop where each item is painstakingly handmade.

OPPOSITE: The products range from clothing to shoes, from blankets to bags, making this the perfect place for gifts.

workshop in Kunshan, a short distance outside Shanghai. Traditional craftsmen and tailors work with meticulous detail creating double sided embroidery and multi-layered cloth shoes (made only on sunny days and with rice glue). There's a subtle hint of Chinese influence in every item of Shanghai Trio's unique selection that combines the traditional art of embroidery with contemporary and fresh designs.

Shanghai Trio has participated in exhibitions worldwide and has had a presence in a range of prestigious galleries and shops including the Galeries Lafayette and Le Bon Marché in Paris and Isetan in Japan. Their creations have a permanent home in China and Taiwan's finest hotels and they are now exporting products to Switzerland, Italy, Spain and France. With reviews in *Elle*, *Elle Deco*, *Wallpaper*, *Marie Claire* and *Madame Figaro Japan*, Shanghai Trio's brand is becoming an increasingly familiar name.

PHOTOGRAPHS COURTESY OF SHANGHAI TRIO.

FACTS

PRODUCTS	gifts • bags • purses • clothing • jewellery • home ware •
FEATURES	Chinese modern and colourful materials • embroidery
NEARBY	Xintiandi (boutique) • French Concession (showroom)
CONTACT	Xintiandi Boutique, Lane 181 Taicang Road, Shanghai, 200021 • telephone: +86.21.6355 2974 • Showroom (closed on weekends) House 6, Lane 37 Fuxing West Road, Shanghai, 200031 • telephone: +86.21.6433 8901 • facsimile: +86.21.6473 7819 • email: shanghaitrio@shanghaitrio.com.cn • website: www.shanghaitrio.com

Shanghart Gallery

Shanghart Gallery is one of the oldest independent art spaces in China. Established in 1996, its first exhibition was displayed on a few walls in a Shanghai hotel. Sixty-six exhibitions later, it is recognized as Shanghai's premier independent art gallery and was the first to participate in major international art fairs.

It has recently taken over a large warehouse in an old textile factory near Suzhou Creek, a fast developing area housing a great proportion of the city's galleries. Commandeering nearly 1,200 sq m (12,900 sq ft), the space itself is a piece of art. Immense in size and height, starkly finished in concrete, whitewashed walls and a vast wooden roof, the exhibition space and gallery still resembles the warehouse it once was. The ability to wander through with such ease, whilst admiring unfinished paintings that have been laid on the floor, or propped up against the impressive works of art hanging on the walls, gives a sense of self-discovery rather than the usual ordered formality.

The gallery represents 30 artists, and the aim is to identify and promote, both locally and internationally, artists who are at the core of artistic creativity in China. And, although there is a special focus on artists living and working in Shanghai, it also represents artists from all over China.

These include Wu Yiming, born in Shanghai in 1966, his works (mainly portraits of sorts) pay homage to both the spiritual world of the ancients and, at the same time, the rapid economic development of the city he grew up in. Less traditional is Zhao Bandi, who graduated from the

...a sense of self-discovery rather than the usual ordered formality.

Central Acadamy of Fine Arts in Beijing whose work has been exhibited around the world including London, Paris, Venice, New York and Berlin. His most recent series of photographic work is in the form of posters with strip-cartoon text. Wang Guangyi, whose recent work has focused on the classical figures of propaganda used in the Cultural Revolution, is the most important representative of China's 'Political Pop', which came to prominence in the early 1990s.

Covering such a huge range of contexts and styles, the gallery conveys a highly diverse picture of both new and old China whilst its impressive setting provides an exciting backdrop. As much for the wildly differentiating works of art, the frequent, dynamic exhibitions and the overwhelming space itself, Shanghart Gallery is a rewarding place to visit for anyone with the slightest interest in art, architecture or a desire to see something different.

FACTS		
PRODUCTS	paintings • sculptures • pieces of art
FEATURES	regular exhibitions • dynamic gallery space
NEARBY	Suzhou Creek
CONTACT	50 Moganshan Road, Building 16 + 18, Shanghai, 200060 • telephone: +86.21.6359 3923 • facsimile: +86.21.6359 4570 • email: info@shanghartgallery.com • website: www.shanghartgallery.com

PHOTOGRAPHS COURTESY OF SHANGHART GALLERY.

Simply Life

Owned by Simply the Group, a company that has triumphed across Shanghai with authentic Thai restaurants (Simply Thai), designer florist Simply Flowers and catering group the Party People—the Simply Life chain of lifestyle stores enjoys the same thriving success as its siblings.

Launched on a quiet road in the French Concession, Simply Life became an instant success, starting an interior design trend across Shanghai. Prior to its opening in 2000, most of the quality home ware produced in China was made for export only and was unavailable to the growing number of resident consumers. Simply the Group's founder, Singapore-born Choon, recognized the demand, and today Shanghai boasts two Simply Life boutiques with plans for more to open soon.

The flagship store is located in fashionable Xintiandi, standing proudly alongside Shanghai Tang, Benetton and Häagen Dazs, its smart image reflects the quality of the goods inside. The original outlet, situated on a small leafy lane not far from the famous shopping malls on Huaihai Road, continues to sell a selected range of distinctive pottery, chinaware and glassware. Simply Life products can also be found at selected five-star hotels around the city.

Likened to the Conran stores—but with a distinctly Asian twist—Simply Life offers not only beautiful top-quality interior design products but also a fresh and spacious environment in which you can leisurely browse. Using clean lines and imaginative

THIS PAGE: *The elegant Asianera product range offers a fresh and contemporary take on the traditions of fine Chinese porcelain.*
OPPOSITE: *The bold design of the shop is the perfect backdrop to the bold designs on sale.*

displays, chic, contemporary designs sit companionably alongside more traditional Asian artefacts. A stunning range of both simple and extravagant vases are displayed on modern glass shelves, gadgets and designer electrical items are cased in spotless glass cabinets while smaller items, ranging from chop-sticks to photo frames, sit decoratively on tables draped in soft silk. The English-speaking staff are friendly and helpful, yet unobtrusive. All these small details, combined with the array of home décor products, create an exciting, and ultimately pleasurable, shopping experience.

Originally selling only local Chinese products, Simply Life has broadened its range, offering a varied selection of world-recognized brands whilst continuing to promote and sell top-quality Chinese home décor goods. Simply Life is especially proud of the Asianera range, created by Shanghai-based Grace Liu. Asianera fine bone china is a new generation of fine china, one that maintains the traditions of technique but adds

is inspired by Shanghai doorframes; the clean, pared down lines of another set reference the distinctive art deco style.

In addition to Asianera, brands now available at Simply Life include Alessi, Riedel, La Cafetière, Umbra, Rosendahl and Dragon World, with products ranging from designer toothpick holders to sophisticated wine holders. The range of local products include beautifully hand embroidered tissue boxes, exquisite evening bags and pieces of ornately painted bone china. Stunning and vivid lacquer ware, part of the Asianoble label, is specially imported from Vietnam, where it has been handcrafted using ancient techniques including hand polishing to provide an exquisite finish. A simple

a contemporary spin—much like modern China itself. Designs are conceived by designer, Li Jianping, with input from Liu, and executed by Chinese artists who, because of their training, make even traditional Western designs look somehow Chinese.

Asianera porcelain also tweaks traditional shapes, drawing upon jewellery, furniture, and even architecture for inspiration: the angular handle of one teapot

THIS PAGE (FROM TOP): The two-storey flagship shop in Xintiandi; inside, the store's arrangement ensures a pleasurable browse.

OPPOSITE (FROM LEFT): The unique cushions make perfect gifts; beautiful lacquer ware is imported from Vietnam; Simply's glass ware, all of exceptional quality.

lacquer item can take a painstaking 75 days to produce with over 18 stages involved; it is certainly worth spending some time to really study the beautiful examples Simply Life has on offer.

Simply Life offers all kinds of interior furnishings and is well stocked to kit out your bathroom, kitchen, sitting room or bedroom. Bedlinen ranges from earthy natural tones to vivid, colourful silks and, as you would expect, all are of the finest quality. Similarly, cushions of varying colours, textures and sizes are hand finished with exceptional care and will add a refined, sophisticated touch to any room. Lamps are available in a variety of sizes and designs, and range from traditionally glazed Chinese lamps to sleek, contemporary chrome spotlights that will suit both the old and new. Kitchenware includes everything from bright and funky Alessi corkscrews and the latest designer gadgets to authentic lacquer chopsticks and other practical accessories. All are unique and rarely seen elsewhere in the city.

The Simply Life selection is both varied and substantial and takes into consideration tastes that are sophisticated and eccentric as well as those that are a little bit different. Whether you're looking for the practical or the fabulous, for yourself or for a gift, at Simply Life you'll be able to find simply everything.

FACTS

PRODUCTS	home ware • appliances • glassware • vases • ceramics • bedlinen
FEATURES	peaceful shopping environment • wide range of choice
NEARBY	Xintiandi • French Concession
CONTACT	Corner of Ma Dang Road and Xing Ye Road, Shanghai, 200021 • telephone: +86.21.6326 2088 • facsimile: +86.21.6384 6522 • 9 Dong Ping Road , Shanghai, 200031 • telephone: +86.21.3406 0509 • facsimile: +86.21.3406 5509 • email: enquiry@simplylife-sh.com • website: www.simplylife-sh.com

PHOTOGRAPHS COURTESY OF SIMPLY LIFE.

Three on the Bund

Art, culture, food, fashion and music are the key concepts behind Three on the Bund's groundbreaking transformation. The first privately owned company to obtain government approval to develop a building on the Bund, Three on the Bund employed world-famous architect Michael Graves to restore the neoclassical building to its former grandeur. Cited by *TIME* magazine as 'the best place to see new China', it boasts four of Shanghai's best restaurants, an Evian spa, exclusive retail outlets, and showcases China's leading contemporary artists at the Shanghai Gallery of Art.

Once a bell tower, the two-storey dome at the top of the building now houses Cupola, the smallest and most intimate restaurant in Shanghai. Downstairs, a dining room for eight people is the perfect location for a dinner party and the room upstairs—with a domed 8-m (26-ft)-high ceiling, 360° view of the city and a table and divan for two—is possibly the most romantic restaurant in the world. A private butler is on hand and guests can select from some of the most exclusive menus in Shanghai including Laris, Whampoa Club and Jean Georges. Alternatively they can create their own menu by combining dishes from all three outlets. Cupola is a truly special experience.

Jean-Georges Vongerichten has many accolades, not least his mention in *Food and Wine* as one of the '10 hottest chefs alive'. Having turned his attentions to Shanghai to open what he described as the favourite of his many worldwide restaurants,

Jean Georges at Three on the Bund is gaining similar appreciation from reviewers—the *International Herald Tribune* considers it the 'most-must-see restaurant'. In the open kitchen chefs create innovative dishes using only the best locally grown, organic produce and the freshest seafood. The design is inspired by the grandeur of Old Shanghai with a French influence. While the bar area is sleek and lively, the dining room embodies a softer, more luxuriant ambience with tall windows looking out onto the river. With over 5,000 bottles of wine in the cellar, every consideration has been made to ensure an enjoyable afternoon or evening.

On the 5th floor, Whampoa Club offers a dramatic dining experience with an unusual slant on Shanghainese cuisine. With a dazzling ceiling to floor chandelier and luminous green, red and blue strip lighting across the restaurant, the reflections on the highly polished wooden floor are stunningly vivid. The food, created by one of Asia's

THIS PAGE (FROM TOP): *Laris Restaurant displays its fresh yet soothing ambience; signature dishes from Jean Georges include the crab with avocado salsa and lemongrass gazpacho and the egg caviar.*

OPPOSITE: *The stunning atrium of the Shanghai Gallery of Art cuts through the building.*

youngest and most renowned master chefs, Jereme Leung, reworks traditional classical recipes—from Shanghai and across China— with a contemporary interpretation. The presentation is equally considered and each dish looks as beautiful as it tastes. The striking tableware by Asianera, custom-made for Whampoa, includes jade plateware, ceramic, porcelain, glass and stone. The overall effect provides a spectacular treat for all your senses.

Laris, on the 6th floor, as with all the restaurants in Three on the Bund, has spectacular views of the Bund. Here David Laris showcases his true passion and flair with tantalizing treats such as Seared Scallops on Parsnip Mash with Oyster Lemon Foam. The main dining room is a soothing space, with soft tones of white on white and exceptionally comfortable seating. Overhead the lighting is a collaboration of alabaster stone and silk fabric, which creates a delightful billowing effect. This serene gentleness is contrasted with the bright lights of Shanghai that peer in through the vast windows.

Just off the main dining area is the Vault Bar. With its gold ceiling and dramatic stone and velvet walls, the bar is a real treasure. The imaginative cocktails and enticing range of appetizers are complemented by a bar menu of delicious snacks and a games menu that includes backgammon or chess.

On the top of the seven-floored building is the appropriately named New Heights which enjoys some of the best views of Shanghai. With its casual atmosphere, brasserie-style interior and glass walls, it has a lively yet relaxed bustle that welcomes people throughout the day and well into the night for meals, snacks, coffee and drinks. Hearty English breakfasts, gourmet burgers and fish and chips are on offer as well as contemporary Asian specialities. An impressive terrace offers unprecedented views and is an exhilarating position from which to enjoy Shanghai by day and night.

Third Degree is a sophisticated music lounge featuring a premium wine and liquor list, tasty late night snacks and great entertainment. Live performances include jazz, contemporary Chinese fusion and acoustic guitar from artists of local and international acclaim.

A white stone bar and tones of deep red and velvety midnight blue create a seductive and luxurious atmosphere, while plush banquettes invite extreme relaxation. In addition to the lounge area, there is also a terrace that seats up to 10 people. This verandah is an idyllic spot for a late night cognac or a glass of champagne under the stars as the Bund stretches out before you.

The Evian Spa Shanghai is a haven for relaxation and rejuvenation. The stunning 35-m (115-ft)-high atrium entrance leads to the 14 individually designed spa rooms. The comprehensive and advanced choices include a range of French beauty treatments, an Indian head massage, a pregnancy massage, a hot stone massage and even a hydrotherapy bath where programmed jets provide underwater massage whilst coloured lights inside the bath stimulate and soothe your body and mind. For men, there's

Barbers by Three. Customers are given a private cubicle, each equipped with a chic black leather barber's chair, a television and a CD/DVD player. Shaves, haircuts, facial treatments, ear candling, manicures, and traditional Shanghainese pedicures, as well as neck and shoulder rubs can all be enjoyed over a fine malt whiskey.

In a stunning space filled with natural light, wooden floors and stone walls, Three Retail offers an exhilarating range of clothing and accessories from around the world. The meticulously curated collection includes couture giants such as Yves Saint Laurent and smaller, ultra-exclusive labels like Ann Demeulemeester and styles vary from the bohemian chic of Marni to the sophisticated high-tech sportswear of C.P. Company. Three Retail also has a selection of in-house designers creating cutting edge designs.

THIS PAGE (FROM LEFT): The Evian Spa, the first in Asia, is a zen-like sanctuary; Three Retail offers the best of designer goods.
OPPOSITE: The Third Degree, a great venue for a night of sophistication. Guests are treated to live performances, premium wines and liquors.

With an atrium that extends from the third floor to the roof, Shanghai Gallery of Art is at the heart of Three on the Bund. From the restaurants above you can look down into the core of the gallery ensuring its central focus. The gallery is becoming increasingly revered and is now considered one of the most noteworthy galleries in Asia. The gallery presents groundbreaking projects such as Oscar winning composer Tan Dun's first solo show. In the stark and exposed space Michael Graves has used raw materials such as metal walls, overhead piping and industrial style lighting to create an inspiring environment.

As development continues and exclusive brands fight their way down to the riverfront, Three On the Bund will remain the pioneer behind the re-growth of the Bund, which has been returned it to its deserved significance and importance in the city. As such Three on the Bund sits firmly at the forefront of Shanghai's glamour.

PHOTOGRAPHS COURTESY OF THREE ON THE BUND.

FACTS

FOOD	Jean Georges • Whampoa Club • Laris • New Heights • The Cupola
DRINK	Third Degree • The Vault at Laris
FEATURES	Three Retail plus other retail outlets • Shanghai Gallery of Art • Evian Spa • Barbers by Three • exclusive dining and retail with spectacular views of the Bund
NEARBY	the Bund • Huangpu River
CONTACT	Jean Georges: +86.21.6321 7733 • Whampoa Club: +86.21.6321 3737 • Laris: +86.21.6321 9922 • New Heights: +86.21.6321 0909 • Evian Spa: +86.21.6321 6622 • Barbers By Three: +86.21.6321 6622 • Shanghai Gallery of Art: +86.21.6321 5757 • Three Retail: +86.21.6321 0101 • email: info@on-the-bund.com • website: www.threeonthebund.com

Xintiandi

Shanghai's distinctive shikumen houses, meaning 'stone-gate homes', feature huge, solid black painted doors and massive stone doorframes whose size was indicative of the owner's status. This characteristic Shanghainese architecture first emerged in the 1860s and as urban living grew more and more dense, the demand for economic shikumen homes expanded and for over a century they dominated the city. Although 2 million people still live in traditional shikumen houses, development continues to threaten their survival and as more and more new buildings reach the futuristic skyline, this cultural heritage of Shanghai is under threat.

In response to this, Hong Kong-based Shui On Group completed their development of Xintiandi in 2002, restoring a traditional shikumen community into an urban tourist attraction. Recognizing the city's thirst for designer boutiques and upmarket bars and restaurants with the cultural and historical legacies of Shanghai, they created a new hub in the city, evocative of Covent Garden in London.

Split into two blocks separated by Xing Le Road, the historic site of the first Congress Hall of the Communist Party, the North block consists of immaculately restored shikumen houses, with original brickwork, tiled roofs and the stone framed, heavy black doors remain. Inside you can find traditional dark wood flooring and the stunning workmanship of the open roof and wooden columns. The South block consists of

THIS PAGE (FROM TOP): Chic restaurants and boutiques line the narrow lanes of Xintiandi; old and new combine and all establishments make good use of their old-world environment.

OPPOSITE (FROM TOP): Xintiandi buzzes with late-night shoppers and bar hoppers and music booms from each venue; street sellers line the pedestrian lanes and contribute to the stylish shopping experience.

essentially modern architecture designed with a sympathetic eye to the old homes. Within the development is the Shikumen Museum where you can walk around an original shikumen home gaining a feel for the traditional layout and the way of life.

However, it's the many bars, restaurants and upmarket boutiques that attract most people to the bustling lanes of Xintiandi. Encompassing everything from famous fashion labels to local jewellery designers and the traditional Zishaware sculptures at Changqingteng, Xintiandi is host to a range of exclusive shops. The lanes are brimming with sophisticated Western and Chinese restaurants with some of the city's most respected chefs and exclusive hangouts. Bars are in abundance with sophisticated jazz exuding from CJW to frenetic live punk rock booming at ARK. Whether you're stopping for a coffee at Starbucks, a burger at Kabb or a cocktail at Latina, if it's at Xintiandi it's certain to be a chic experience.

PHOTOGRAPHS COURTESY OF XINTIANDI.

FACTS

PRODUCTS	fashion • jewellery • accessories • gifts • homeware • cinema • bank • 88 Xintiandi Hotel • hairdressers • health and fitness club • information centre • museum • gallery
FOOD	Western • Chinese
DRINK	numerous bars
FEATURES	attractive tourist development with shops • bars • restaurants
NEARBY	Huaihai Road • People's Square
CONTACT	North Block: Lane 181 Taicang Road, Shanghai, 200021 • South Block: Lane 123 Xing Ye Road, Shanghai, 200021 • telephone: +86.21.6311 2288 • email: info@xintiandi.com • website: www.xintiandi.com

Banyan Tree Spa Shanghai

THIS PAGE: *The Gold Room in which the senses are soothed and treatments are based on purification.*

OPPOSITE (CLOCKWISE FROM LEFT): *In the sumptuous Water Room relaxation is induced by calming sounds of water; the spa's beautiful Wood Room creates the setting for the renewal-based therapy; the main corridor at the Banyan Tree Spa Shanghai where the senses are immediately struck in this sanctuary of well-being.*

In a city where East and West are juxtaposed on every street, where fast-developing futuristic buildings generate a new skyline each month and where more and more people are able to live their lives in penthouse apartments and dine at elite restaurants, it seems fitting that the Banyan Tree has chosen Shanghai to open its pioneering spa incorporating a post-modern approach to treatments. At the Banyan Tree Spa Shanghai, pampering begins the moment you step into the entrance. Soaking up the surroundings—the thick red carpets, gold statues, black lacquer walls and bonsai trees—the stress and mayhem of the city are washed away instantly.

With its signature spa treatments, the Banyan Tree Spa offers a range of packages that relax, refresh, renew and rejuvenate. The real delights are in a new concept of well-being that introduces an ultimately modern approach to the ancient Chinese philosophy of 'Wu Xing'. The time-honoured Five Elements symbolize life forces on earth and are manifestations of the Yin and Yang, the opposing states of nature. Using a combination of treatments mirroring the characteristics of these elements, Earth, Gold, Water, Wood and Fire, Banyan Tree Spa has created unique packages that induce equilibrium and relaxation in accordance with your birth sign.

The first package, Earth, induces balance and is at the centre of Yin and Yang. A Balinese Massage, Lulur Scrub and an Earth Facial treatment improves and distributes the energy flow throughout the body. The second, Gold, represents purification. A Swedish Massage, steam treatment and a Volcanic Purifier Wrap, ensure a deep cleansing process that will draw toxins from the body. For relaxation, the Water package includes a meditative

...pampering begins the moment you step into the impressive entrance.

and refreshing massage, a Sweet Honey Exfoliation and deep skin nourishment that soothes away any aches and pains. For a more invigorating spa treatment, Wood is associated with renewal. Here a Sports Massage, designed to improve muscular strength and flexibility, is followed by further massages and scrubs to stimulate the blood circulation. Finally Fire, the symbol of energy and vitality, combines massages, reflexology and baths to ensure you leave the spa feeling reinvigorated.

The Banyan Tree Spa has tailor-made each suite to reflect one of the five elements. In the cool and tranquil Water Room, water flows calmly into a lotus pond, glass bowls filled with water and flowers sit in niches in the green and blue lit walls. In contrast the Fire Room has copper emblazoned on the walls reflecting the striking candles burning in tall vases rising up from the red floor. This attention to all your senses ensures you'll leave the Banyan Tree Spa feeling light and rejuvenated in both the body and mind.

FACTS		
	ROOMS	13 treatment rooms • 1 beauty salon
	PRODUCTS	facial treatments • full body treatments • hair and beauty treatments • massage • manicures • pedicures
	FEATURES	new concept spa • stunning interior
	NEARBY	the Bund • Huangpu River
	CONTACT	Level 3 The Westin Shanghai, Bund Centre 88 Henan Central Road, Shanghai, 200002 • telephone: +86.21.6335 1888 • facsimile: +86.21.6335 1113 • email: spa-shanghai@banyantree.com • website: www.banyantreespa.com/shanghai

PHOTOGRAPHS COURTESY OF BANYAN TREE SPA SHANGHAI.

Mandara Spa

Nestled within the modern chrome and glass frontage of the JW Marriott Hotel, Mandara's most prestigious spa in Asia provides a sensual and warm contrast to the minimalism of its striking surroundings. Entering through large glass doors the atmosphere immediately softens with rich and vibrant silk lounges, beautiful candles floating on exquisite water features and soft calming music. The soothing scents of aromatherapy and massage oils linger in the air and before the pampering has even begun you can feel your body unwind.

Founded in Bali in 1995 and now boasting spas in both Asia and the Middle East, Mandara Spa has a distinctly Asian influence. The exposed wooden beams, unpolished old bricks and naturally aged uneven floor boards are reminiscent of the traditional Shanghainese Shikumen houses and this thoughtfully considered attention to old Shanghai creates a unique and

characteristic charm. Exotic Indonesian, Thai and Chinese features incorporate rich timbers, oriental ceramics and colourful silks indigenous to the East, enhancing the rich and luxurious setting.

Mandara Spa is a delicate world of relaxation and rejuvenation for both men and women and has a host of spa treatments that are designed to de-stress, renew and balance your body, mind and spirit. Mandara offers suites for couples, friends, or those wishing tranquil solitude.

In harmony with the architecture the treatments themselves are instilled with the beauty and allure of ancient traditions and use historic Asian rituals in health and beauty along with the sophistication of modern spa techniques to provide the ultimate

THIS PAGE: Inspired by Asian traditions the décor creates a serene sanctuary.

OPPOSITE: Situated high up in the JW Marriott Hotel, the entrance to the spa where the warm tones are immediately welcoming.

indulgences. There's a wide range of choice, each treatment is uniquely designed to relax, revitalize and rejuvenate. In a city of temperate extremes Mandara Spa offers equal diversity and you can enjoy treatments that are both cooling and invigorating on the skin and warming and stimulating for the body. In the heat of the summer a traditional Javanese beauty treatment, Javanese Lulur, is a blissful and reviving luxury as it softens, nourishes and refreshes your skin using a blend of powdered spices, sweet woods and cool yoghurt. The Mandarin Spice Aromatherapy massage, with its blend of ginger, cloves and mandarin is a sensual and stimulating way to warm your body and soothe aching bones from the cold.

The word Mandara refers to an ancient Sanskrit myth, the quest to discover the precious elixir of immortality and eternal youth, leaving the tranquil environment of your private suite you certainly feel younger, lighter and energized.

PHOTOGRAPHS COURTESY OF MANDARA SPA.

FACTS		
ROOMS	3 deluxe spa suites • 3 double spa suites • 2 single spa suites • full service beauty salon	
TREATMENT	facial treatments • full body treatments • massage • manicures • pedicures	
FEATURES	private suites • oversized terrazzo bathtubs	
NEARBY	People's Square	
CONTACT	6th Floor, JW Marriott Hotel, Tomorrow Square, 399 Nanjing West Road, Shanghai, 200003 • telephone: +86.21.5359 4969 ext 6798, 6799 • facsimile: +86.21.5852 1155 • email: infochina@minornet.com • website: www.mspa-international.com	

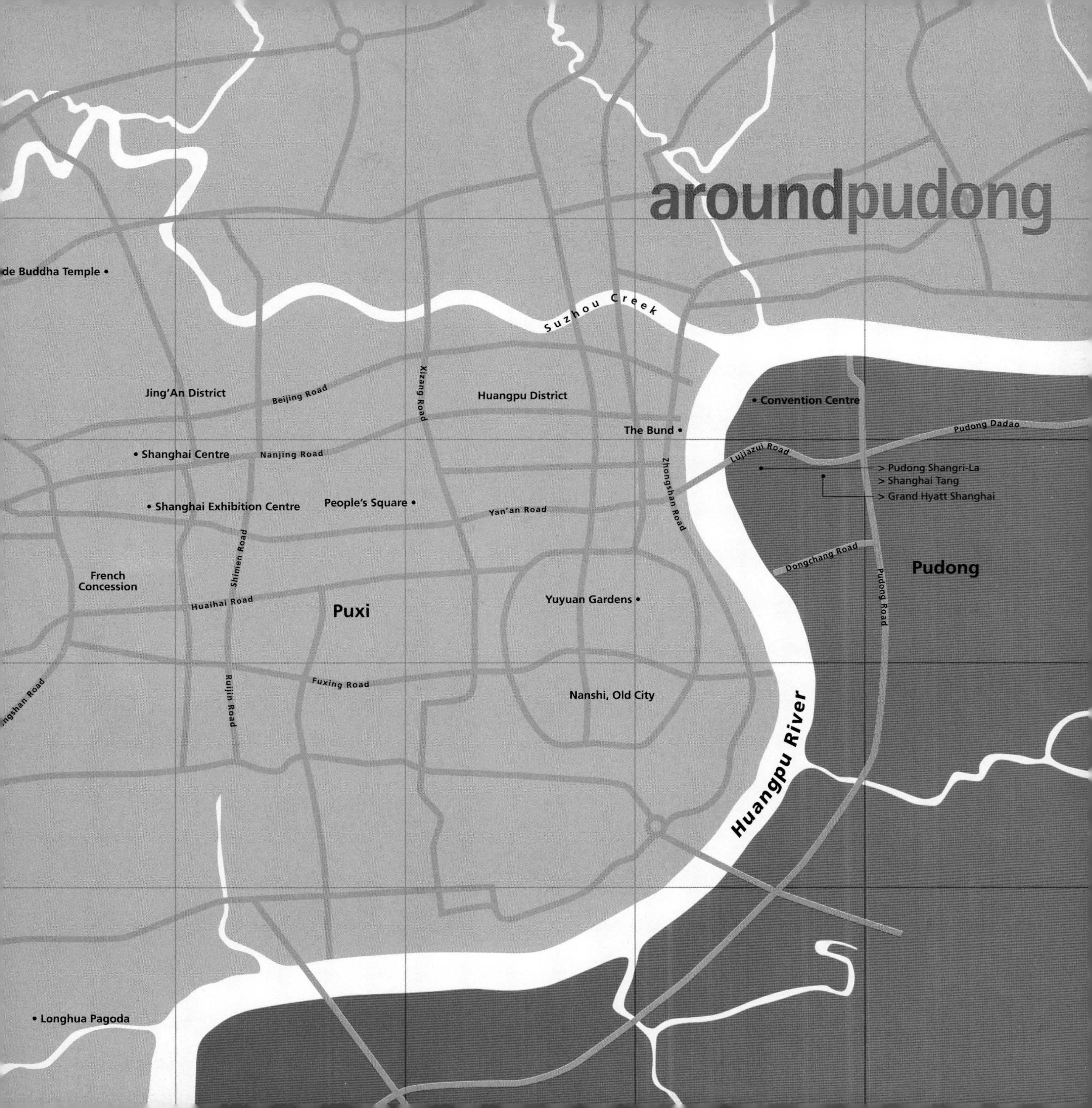

aroundpudong

de Buddha Temple •

Suzhou Creek

Jing'An District

Beijing Road

Xizang Road

Huangpu District

The Bund •

• Convention Centre

Pudong Dadao

Lujiazui Road

• Shanghai Centre

Nanjing Road

Zhongshan Road

> Pudong Shangri-La
> Shanghai Tang
> Grand Hyatt Shanghai

• Shanghai Exhibition Centre

People's Square •

Yan'an Road

Dongchang Road

Pudong

Shimen Road

French
Concession

Huaihai Road

Puxi

Yuyuan Gardens •

Pudong Road

hongshan Road

Ruijin Road

Fuxing Road

Nanshi, Old City

Huangpu River

• Longhua Pagoda

china's powerhouse

The Shanghainese are known for being a proud lot, but, they might argue, they have good reason to be. After all, they are the wealthiest citizens of mainland China. Everyone seems to be coming to Shanghai, or talking about it, after media reports touted it as the world's hottest city. Shanghai has recently earned the distinction of being the busiest port on the planet, handling more millions of tons of cargo in a year than rivals Rotterdam, Hong Kong or Singapore. The municipality's destiny, officially mapped out by Beijing, is to be a foremost international business and financial hub.

Already the Shanghainese economy boggles the mind, its growth spurt as astonishing as the adolescent Yao Ming's. (Yao, a Shanghai-born centre for the NBA's Houston Rockets, is an amazing 2.26 m (7 ft 5 in) tall). In 2004, for instance, the economy shot up an eye-popping 14 per cent over the year before. That's astounding even against the national track record, which is a wowing 8 per cent annual growth over the past couple of decades. Shanghai's gross domestic product (GDP) per capita is 51,500 RMB, nearly five times the nation's average and almost twice that of Beijing's 26,625 RMB. Income per capita in Shanghai is 28,000 RMB, compared to 15,300 RMB in Beijing. Although the metropolis holds slightly more than 1 per cent of the country's 1.3 billion people, it produces 5 per cent of China's total output. The exports it churns out constitute at least 10 per cent of all of China's exports to the rest of the world. And it wins about one-sixth of the contracted foreign direct investment money flowing into the country.

the golden goose

Economics and business haven't always been a cause for civic celebration, however. After taking power in 1949, the Chinese Communist Party also took over all private-sector companies, land and other assets. Following the Soviet Union model, it moulded the economy from a free-wheeling, free-market one into a centrally-planned bureaucracy. Beijing would disseminate sky-high production quotas or sanguine Three-

PAGE 158: The financial district of Pudong houses Shanghai's most modern and impressive towers.

THIS PAGE: Nanpu Bridge, one of the city's important landmarks.

OPPOSITE: Building skyscrapers, bridges, highways and other major infrastructure has been a government priority since the 1990s.

Year Plans or Five-Year Plans, and the cities and provinces would have to jump to try to fulfil them.

Shanghai was known as a fertile golden-egg-laying goose. For one, its location is prime, at the mid-point of China's coast. It abuts both the ocean and the mouth of the Yangzi (China's longest river), a main entrance to the country's sprawling interior. And though it suffered a brain-drain before the Communist take-over, when many elites fled to Hong Kong and Taiwan, Shanghai could still claim to have China's most talented and technically skilled workforce. Its people, whose origins were typically outside the city, were characteristically gutsy and ambitious, with quick wits, steely resiliency and open minds. It had the most extensive infrastructure, the most advanced machinery, and the greatest administrative and logistics know-how. Seagull cameras, Hero pens and other Shanghainese brands had a well-deserved reputation for being the highest quality in the country.

The central government, naturally, knew all about what Shanghai could offer, and took advantage of it. Over the following decades, Beijing siphoned most of Shanghai's revenues and re-distributed them to prop up poor areas of the country. At the same time, Beijing was watchful of the Shanghainese goose because of her notoriously capitalist and unabashedly bourgeois history—so it made sure to fill the top slots in Shanghai's government with non-Shanghainese. After Mao Zedong died in 1976 and the Shanghai-based Gang of Four were arrested, Beijing had new cause to be wary of Shanghai. It put conservative Communist Party stalwarts in charge of the city, whose task was to flush out any leftover Gang of Four sympathizers. Shanghai, then, had little clout in Beijing's inner circles. Yet it was

Beijing's biggest single financer. As much as 80 per cent of its earnings went to the capital, which added up to about one-sixth of the central government's total revenues. Shanghai was also the source of one-quarter of China's exports. In return, Shanghai was granted a miniscule seven per cent of the amount it contributed, to be used for basic construction. With never-ending production targets to meet, the municipal government spent most of that tiny sum on manufacturing instead of less glorious, less hyped sectors such as education and housing.

For three whole decades, the Communist government barricaded China against capitalism and other foreign influences. However, communes and egalitarianism did not transform people into perfect socialist beings; their motivation and productivity were clearly inspired more by incentives and individual autonomy than by political theory.

the gradual opening up

Pragmatic leader Deng Xiaoping opened China's doors in 1979 and charted a new direction. He drew up blueprints for trial 'special economic zones' that would lure foreign capital and expertise with tax breaks, new roads, less red tape and other perks. But experimenting in Shanghai seemed too risky; if it flopped, it might end up cooking the invaluable goose. So instead, Deng designated southern China as the venue for the first special zones. The south began to soar. The Shanghai economy, still closed and mired in state planning and state ownership, stagnated. By the mid-1980s, in industrial output, exports and even consumer loyalty, Shanghai was fast losing ground to other regions of China.

the great turnaround

It is said that in China, business fortunes (or misfortunes) can ride on the quality of one's guanxi (connections) and the level of one's savvy, and that was certainly true with Shanghai's slump in the 1980s and turnaround in the 1990s. The resuscitation began with the entrance of Jiang Zemin and Zhu Rongji, both well-educated, heavy-hitting

THIS PAGE (FROM TOP): Across the 1907 steel Waibaidu Bridge is Shanghai Mansions hotel, built in 1935 as luxury apartments; many of Shanghai's streets await redevelopment.
OPPOSITE: Symbols of confidence and pride on the city's riverfront.

technocrats. Jiang, affable but shrewd, and Zhu, a media darling, were appointed to lead Shanghai in the late 1980s. Armed with high-level connections, they lobbied for Beijing's help in reviving and reforming the city's economy. Their handling of pro-democracy demonstrations in Shanghai in June 1989, which dissipated the protest without force, was exemplary compared to what happened at Beijing's Tiananmen Square. Deng Xiaoping took note and promoted them, anointing Jiang as his successor and picking Zhu to be the nation's premier. They, in turn, recruited Shanghai-connected officials for other central government posts.

In 1992, Deng declared that the future of Shanghai's economy would determine the development of the nation as a whole. (In a rare admission, he also said he'd erred in not including Shanghai in the inaugural special economic zone experiment in 1979.) Shanghai finally had Beijing's support (which would include funding, loans and preferential policies) to launch a slew of economic reforms. It could court foreign banks, multinationals and private enterprises, organize several special zones in Pudong and build industrial parks. Shanghai was back on track—and ready to subject itself to a reconstruction of superhuman proportions.

If there's one thing that visitors to Shanghai in the 1990s remember, it's the dust. The city seemed to be one surreal construction zone. To make way for everything new, ageing factories in Puxi were shifted to outlying areas of the city. Nearly 500,000 households—about one in every 10 in Shanghai—were uprooted and trucked to new accommodation, also on the outskirts.

As apartments and houses had filled up over the decades, residents had been left to devise add-ons and fashion living space under stairways, in hallways and courtyards, on balconies and rooftops. New housing had been long overdue; the city hadn't built any to speak of. Now in the 1990s—relocated hours away from their workplaces and the city centre—families often felt disoriented at first. But at least their new quarters had private flush toilets. For many, it was the first time in their lives that they didn't have to rely on chamber pots.

THIS PAGE: *From Bund 18, a view of glass-and-steel Pudong.*

OPPOSITE (FROM TOP): *River traffic on the bustling Huangpu River; forests of modern apartments are sprouting up in the suburbs.*

The newly-vacated lots were generally not vacant for long. Shanghai's government sold the land-use rights of the residential buildings and old factories to property development companies, many of them from Hong Kong. Betting on an influx of multinational corporations and expatriate executives, the developers began to erect office and apartment towers, shopping and entertainment plazas, and gated communities of lavish villas.

a new shanghai is born

As of the mid-1990s, about 3 million labourers from other provinces were in Shanghai, working on an estimated 21,000 construction sites. Pudong's shiny silver-and-pink monument to modernity, the Oriental Pearl TV Tower, was the tallest structure in Asia when it was finished in 1995. The Jetsons-esque tower was quickly adopted as the icon of New Shanghai. The glittery Shanghai Stock Exchange Building opened two years later. By 2000, a new elevated expressway network and a subway intersected the metropolis, jets buzzed in and out of Pudong's flashy airport, and four suspension bridges spanned the Huangpu River. In 2004, the world's first magnetic levitation train in commercial use began literally levitating passengers from the city to the airport in eight minutes, a journey that's nearly an hour by car.

The construction and infrastructure frenzy is just part of the economic miracle that Shanghai is attempting. Its manufacturers have been updating their product lists to hone in on higher-value goods such as microelectronics and telecom equipment. A mini-Detroit has sprouted in Pudong, with joint-venture plants owned by Volkswagen, General Motors and their Chinese partners that build Santanas (a favourite of Shanghai's cabbies) and Buicks for the domestic market. The first made-in-China Cadillacs are to roll off the assembly lines soon.

Although manufacturing has long been one of the economy's strengths, services—sales, financial, logistical, headhunting, insurance and others—now generate more than half of the city's GDP. Shanghai figures that to become Asia's Wall Street, it must

at least double its number of financial-services professionals (it has 100,000 now, compared to Hong Kong's 350,000 and New York's 770,000). To keep up its status as a prominent harbour, it is digging a deep-water port and constructing a dock specifically for cruise ships. Shanghai, equipped with six cavernous convention sites, is also advertising itself as a perfect host of exhibitions, conferences and trade fairs. In 2005, it accommodated more than 300 such gatherings that focused on niches such as wedding photography, waste treatment, animation, refrigeration and air conditioning, textiles and adult toys.

the foreign presence

Foreign entrepreneurs and companies are not merely parachuting into Shanghai for a few days of plastics-and-rubber conferencing. Many have moved in and set up shop; many more are on the way. (The United States Commercial Service counts more than 4,000 US-invested ventures in Shanghai.) The likes of Siemens, GE, AIG and BASF have invested big. Following the flow of business over the past several years, a steady stream of multinationals has shifted headquarters from Hong Kong and Singapore to Shanghai. IT and pharmaceutical corporations are planting research and development centres in town. The Starwood group plans to operate eight hotels in Shanghai by 2010, including a W and two Sheratons—up from its three hotels in 2005. Thus far, there seems to be no shortage of business. Western and other non-Chinese law offices, public relations firms, consultancies and ad agencies say there's plenty of work to go around and an increasing portion of it is coming from Chinese clients.

moving toward globalization

In joining the World Trade Organization in 2001, China committed itself to globalization, free trade, uniform rules and competition. It pledged to open its market wider, by lowering tariffs on imported cars, computers, food and other products, allowing foreign players in previously closed sectors such as distribution and retailing, and

introducing new regulations for everything from banking to bankruptcy. Shanghai and Beijing set up WTO Affairs Consulting Centres, staffed by experts in law and economics.

China has made notable progress since then, but still faces many hurdles. It has written volumes of laws, but implementation and enforcement are uneven, in part due to a dearth of trained lawyers and judges. Corruption is deep-rooted. Unlawfully copying of trademarked, copyrighted and patented items is common, and not only multinationals but increasingly Chinese manufacturers are finding themselves the victims of intellectual-property pirates.

The dilemma facing Communist Party leaders is how to modernize the economy and achieve prosperity, while maintaining social stability and holding onto their political power. If they pull the plug on too many ailing and obsolete state-owned businesses, or if Chinese companies can't withstand foreign competition, the result would be massive lay-offs. Widespread unemployment—coupled with the cuts in state-provided health care, housing and other social benefits—would mean public disgruntlement and tension.

world expo host

One of Shanghai's latest glories is its winning bid to host the World Expo, the third-largest event and spectacle in the world (after the Olympics and the World Cup). In being crowned the 2010 Expo host, Shanghai broke ground: never before has a developing country been selected. Constructing the expo site in Pudong is estimated to cost US$3 billion—and more than half of the budget is earmarked for evacuating and relocating residents. Among the items on the to-do list are: build assorted national pavilions and yet another convention centre; spiff up the banks of the Huangpu River; and lay a new tram line. The Expo will also benefit from another US$48 billion that's already being spent on infrastructure projects slated to benefit Shanghai in the long-run, including expanding the subway system, Pudong airport's terminals and the supply of clean drinking water.

THIS PAGE (FROM TOP): *Shanghai International Convention Centre; Shanghai's subway takes thousands of relocated residents to work in the city-centre.*

OPPOSITE: *The Huangpu continues to be a hard-working river.*

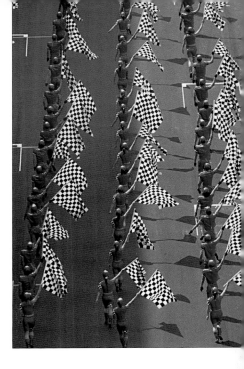

shanghai today

Shanghai is in the midst of a forward-looking revolution to retrieve what it had in the past: prestige as the Asian capital of business, trade, high society and high culture. Since the 1990s, it has been on a building spree which has produced most of the landmarks at People's Square, a new airport, the financial district of Pudong and China's biggest stock exchange, new parks and other green spaces, and renovations and re-openings of historic Bund edifices. In a mere two years it built on a swamp what Michael Schumacher called 'the best racetrack I have ever seen', for China's first Formula One Grand Prix, held in 2004. Besides hosting the F1 for the next several years, Shanghai is staging the global Special Olympics in 2007 and the World Expo in 2010. Several hotels are under construction, including a six-star Peninsula at the north end of the Bund. Suzhou Creek and its embankments, now commonly used to transport and process garbage and recyclables, will be cleaned up. To ease the population density and congestion in central Shanghai, by 2020, 11 satellite cities are to be developed, along with subway and railway lines to put each of the new cities within a one-hour commute of Shanghai.

All of this activity has piqued worldwide interest. Foreigners, especially overseas Chinese, have swarmed to Shanghai for business; some 300,000 Taiwanese are living here. Citizens of the Chinese mainland are returning from stints of studying or working abroad, eager to grab a part of the revolution—more than 90 per cent have advanced degrees, and about one-third of all returnees have chosen to settle back in Shanghai. Chinese from other provinces come to pick up construction and domestic jobs. As it was before 1949, Shanghai is once again a beacon of opportunity and energy.

return of chic shanghai

And it is again China's trendiest city. Heaps of disposable income have given birth to a must-have list like that in the West: home-ownership, Cuban cigars, custom interior design, mistresses and gigolos, tattoos, wine-tasting dinners, modern Chinese art

THIS PAGE (FROM TOP): *F1 fanfare; the F1 racetrack was built atop a swamp in a mere two years.*

OPPOSITE: *Shanghai will host the Special Olympics, scheduled for October 2007. The event will bring more than 7,000 athletes from 150 nations to the city.*

collections, Chihuahuas and toy poodles in jewelled collars, SUVs. China has an established reputation for being a nation of savers, but Shanghai now is a tornado of consumption, and the more conspicuous, the better. Shanghai couples and their parents throw weddings that cost an average of US$19,000 (including the rings, photography and banquets), more than triple the cost three years ago. In the spring of 2005, CEOs of splurge—from the likes of Bulgari, Prada, Giorgio Armani and Richemont—gathered at a luxury-brands conference in Shanghai to pay tribute to China as their next big frontier. The following month in Shanghai, 3,000 local executives and individuals each worth at least US$1 million were invited to an exclusive showcase of cognac, private planes and hedonistic products by Lamborghini, Feadship and Bovet.

the future: bullish and bearish

Incessant jack-hammering, cranes on the horizon, restaurants requiring reservations, bustling hotel lobbies, more foreign language chatter everywhere—it's easy to come to a bullish conclusion about Shanghai's future. Some businesspeople have high expectations and are anticipating double-digit annual growth over the next decade or longer. Real estate developers rhapsodize about the fabulous "upside potential".

No such torrent of modernization is trouble-free, however. Rifts between the younger and older generations have begun to appear. Shanghai's young people, nearly all of them single children because of the government's one-child policy, are focused on materialism and satisfying themselves. They crave individuality, independence, privacy and the best of everything. If they can afford to, they move out of their parents' home. They're relatively liberal with sex. Communism is irrelevant to them. (One e-newsletter of parties around town has the cheeky motto 'It's a communist country: share the party knowledge'.)

The economic boom has also brought energy shortages, property speculation, corruption, and prostitutes and beggars. Shanghai's government woefully underestimated the explosion in automobile traffic, which frequently turns the air grey with pollution. Lay-offs have hit as the government tries to reform and sell off its state-owned companies. In this nominally Communist and egalitarian country, the overriding problem has become the yawning income gap, which is reminiscent of Shanghai during the 1920s and 1930s.

Indeed, someone who saw Shanghai then might feel a little déjà vu now. The municipality has the same sorts of international residents, architecture, fashion-sense, jazz scene, buzz and dark undersides that it had before 1949. Dancers in high-slit qipaos are rumba-ing and foxtrotting once again in the popular Art Deco Paramount Ballroom, one of the city's premier nightlife spots in the 1930s. Private clubs and tipping are in vogue. Western expatriates once again hire domestic servants and prefer living in the former French Concession. Bars, restaurants, dress shops, movies, home décor stores, advertisements, music and art galleries are all working hard to invoke Shanghai's golden era.

a modern personality

Despite the active romanticism and the many plaudits it receives, Shanghai today is not the Shanghai of the 1930s. Back then, it was an oasis surrounded by various vying governments, warlords and rebels. Foreigners ruled and did as they pleased in their concession territories. Now the Communist government, responsible for maintaining social stability, has broad control over the economy. It favours its own state enterprises and tends to be biased against the private sector when it comes to things such as bank loans and enforcing regulations. In addition, Shanghai now has plenty of rivals. For investment, imaginative brainpower, state-of-the-art technology, entrepreneurial spirit and foreign expertise, it is competing with other prominent Chinese and Asian cities such as Beijing, Guangzhou, Shenzhen, Hong Kong and Singapore.

THIS PAGE: *Shanghai swings once again, ballroom dancing has returned to the Paramount.*

OPPOSITE (FROM TOP): *The lanes of Xintiandi play host to many of the world's favourite brands; luxury goods companies are betting on Shanghai.*

Shanghai's prosperity and modernity aren't as deep as they appear. In gleaming malls of Louis Vuitton, Gucci, Cartier, Chanel and Zegna boutiques, most shoppers are purely window-shopping. The Shanghai Stock Exchange sits in a magnificent home in Pudong, but is riddled with speculation, scandal and government intervention. Out-of-town dignitaries tend to get a spiffed-up version of the city; during the 1999 Fortune Global Forum and the 2001 APEC conference, the motorcade routes were lined with flower boxes and strings of coloured lights. There is also outright trompe-l'oeil: the brick façade of a lilong may look freshly scrubbed, but a closer inspection might reveal that it's been covered by a coat of thick grey paint and then white rectangles painted to look like individual bricks. Inside, the living conditions remain poor. Shanghai is the most crowded of China's municipalities and provinces and its property prices are the highest.

Though accustomed to being No. 1 in the nation (in mostly positive aspects), Shanghai has a long way to go before it can claim to be the New York of Asia. Unfortunately, glowing statements from the government, business circuit and media, added to the thick nostalgia for Shanghai's glory days, have been repeated and exaggerated enough that expectations have morphed into unrealistic dimensions. People are lapping up the hype. They perceive Shanghai's changing skyline as a barometer of present reality in Shanghai, rather than of future potential. But the metropolis needs some time to grow into its skyline. To be a global superstar, a city also needs its own modern personality, and while Shanghai has expertly milked nostalgia and racked up superlatives, that does not substitute for a distinguishing contemporary character.

As it has shown just since 1990, the city above the sea is capable of truly Herculean accomplishments. Its ambitions are bold, even grandiose. In ten, five, and even two years hence, in both form and personality, Shanghai will likely look different from the way it does today. Given its unstoppable confidence and optimism, though, it will no doubt be happening and chic.

THIS PAGE: *Window shopping is a favourite pastime in the trendiest city of China.*
OPPOSITE: *The old is readily demolished to make way for the new.*

...it will no doubt be happening and chic.

shanghainese style emergence

No other place on earth has such a mélange of architectural styles as Shanghai. German Renaissance, Tudor, Turkish, Gothic, Spanish Colonial, Art Deco, Mediterranean, Italianate, French and Shanghainese—they're all here, concrete proof of the city's historic cosmopolitanism. The world's refugees and immigrants flocked to Shanghai and built homes, workplaces and communities, never imagining that their occupancy or ownership might be only temporary.

From 1941 until the end of the war, when Japan was in control of the entire city, construction basically came to a halt. That remained the case after the 1949 Communist revolution too, as the Communist Party distributed the city's wealth to poorer areas of the country. As the population ballooned, Shanghai's buildings were increasingly stuffed, added onto and subdivided. Many architectural gems were damaged or destroyed during the Cultural Revolution, as the Red Guards were free to rampage against anything that was Western, bourgeois or traditional.

In the early 1990s, the central government finally gave Shanghai the go-ahead to embark on economic development. The city has taken the endorsement and run with it like an athlete on steroids and in the process, whole neighbourhoods have been bulldozed to make way for high-rises and parks.

traditional styles

For a glimpse of traditional Chinese architecture, head to Yuyuan Gardens in the Old City. The Ming Dynasty-style buildings (most of them are modern-day reconstructions) have tile roofs that swoop upward at their corners, whitewashed walls and latticework. On Fangbang Road are several wood-panelled houses built in the early 1900s. Just as 100 years ago, several have shops on the ground level and living space above.

The most iconic form of native-Shanghai architecture is the lilong or longtang, a walled-off block of rows and rows of housing with narrow, semi-public alleyways running between them. As Chinese refugees continued to pour into Shanghai's foreign

THIS PAGE (FROM TOP): *Attention to detail is considered in modern, just as they were in the old buildings of Shanghai; the elaborate door frames of the traditional stone gate homes.*
OPPOSITE: *Inside the impressive Shanghai Exhibition Centre.*

enclaves through the early 1900s, seeking sanctuary from the fighting between the imperial government and rebels (and later the civil war), Western entrepreneurs realized there was a need for (and a potential fortune in) housing. The lilong was designed to fit lots of people in a limited space, and thus maximize profits. The lane neighbourhoods became tightly-knit communities where virtually nothing went unnoticed. Each house's entrance opened directly into a lane, where adults would come out to gossip, play cards, scrub clothes or shell beans and kids would play ball.

The houses were typically shikumen (literally 'stone-gate house'), named after their doorways. The entrance was a wooden door framed by three stone slabs, often stylishly carved, which led to a small and enclosed courtyard and then the living quarters. Thus, the shikumen had an air of security, solemnity and exclusiveness.

A shikumen was initially meant for one family. The houses were quickly subdivided, however, as the city's population burgeoned. Nowadays it's not uncommon to find five, eight or 10 families in one shikumen, sharing a stove inside and an outdoor sink or tap. Because space was at a premium, courtyards were soon omitted during construction—or families expropriated them and turned them into rooms. Often floors were added on top of the roof. Most shikumen still lack indoor plumbing and running water, so residents continue to rely on chamber pots. About 60 per cent of today's Shanghainese grew up in shikumen. Due to the metropolis' frantic tearing down and building up lately, shikumen now amount to only about one-fifth of their number in 1949. Most are in the Jing'An, Huangpu and Hongkou sections of town.

concession-era cosmopolitanism

Shanghai's signature concession-era architecture resulted from an extraordinary explosion of growth and building over a short time span. Although foreigners never accounted for more than 10 per cent of Shanghai's total population, they dominated politically and economically. Thus they were able to leave an indelible imprint on the city that was disproportionate to their numbers. Making an especially deep impression on Shanghai was Palmer and Turner. On the Bund, the British architectural firm was behind several of the stately structures, including the leader of the Bund, the neoclassical Hong Kong and Shanghai Bank building (now the Pudong Development Bank). Palmer and Turner also designed the Customs House next door, the Peace Hotel, and the buildings now called Three on the Bund and Bund 18. At Jiangxi Road and Fuzhou Road, the firm was responsible for twin high-rises across the street from each other, which originally contained plush apartments.

Ladislaus Hudec, a Czech refugee who arrived in Shanghai in 1918, was another prolific architect. His buildings include: the brick Normandie, which has an inviting, front curve and resembles New York City's Flatiron building; the Shanghai Arts and Crafts Museum, one of the most lavish mansions in the French Concession, which was built for a French official and later became the residence of Shanghai's first Communist mayor; the 1934 Park Hotel on Nanjing Road, which was topped by a nightclub with a retractable roof and which inspired the eminent China-born architect I.M. Pei; the American Club, which boasted an 'American Georgian colonial' style and imported American bricks and is now the People's Court; the Moore Memorial Church, which has textured brickwork; an Art Deco manor on Tongren Road now occupied by the Shanghai City Planning Institute; and the Grand Theatre, considered the Far East's finest cinema when it opened in 1933.

In the former French Concession and International Settlement, Art Deco, Chicago, Mediterranean, neoclassical and Tudor styles are on display. The British Morriss family, whose wealth was built on publishing and casinos, owned a block-long estate with English manors which was

THIS PAGE: The Peace Hotel, one of Palmer and Turner's distinctive buildings that marks Shanghai's cityscape.

OPPOSITE (FROM TOP): Crammed housing built pre-1949; the leafy lanes of the elegant French Concession.

conveniently adjacent to the family-run dog racetrack. (The compound now has restaurants and the Ruijin Guesthouse.) Hengshan, Gao An, Yongfu and Fuxing are just some of the roads dotted with the former stately villas of tycoons, politicians and top mobsters and the art-deco-accented apartments where middle-class and professional expatriates and Chinese lived.

preservation and innovation

The past couple of decades have seen some efforts in Shanghai to preserve rather than demolish and to combine bold creativity with Chinese elements. Along the Bund, designers consulted the original blueprints and photos of the aged building at No. 18 to plan its restoration. After painstaking clean-up and much handiwork, the building reopened with luxury shops and restaurants. The 1998 Shanghai Grand Theatre, designed by Jean-Marie Charpentier of France, is a sleek study in white and glass but its curved roof mimics that of a traditional Chinese pagoda. Shanghai Centre on Nanjing Road, which contains the Portman Ritz-Carlton Hotel, is shaped like the Chinese character shan, or mountain. And there's precedent-setting Xintiandi, near the site of the first Chinese Communist Party congress, which has made shikumen trendy. Taking two square-blocks of shikumen, the developer razed the interiors and kept some of the old grey façades and doorframes to create an upmarket shopping and entertainment complex.

Pudong has a more theatrical if not ostentatious air, with the Oriental Pearl TV Tower's pink and silver balls, the gold Aurora slab that flashes video clips and messages after dark, and the giant globes flanking the Shanghai International Convention Centre. The Lupu Bridge toward the south has the longest arched span in the world—553 m (1,815 ft). Next to the Jin Mao Tower is the site of the 101-storey Shanghai World Financial Centre. Had it met its original completion date in 2004, it would have been the world's tallest building, but funding problems stalled the project. It's now scheduled to be finished in 2007, but it will be 17 m (55 ft) shorter than the current record-holder, the Taipei Financial Centre in Taiwan.

THIS PAGE: Pudong continues to expand while millions of migrant workers contribute to Shanghai's construction boom.
OPPOSITE: Love-it-or-hate-it Oriental Pearl TV Tower, up close.

...concrete proof of the city's historic cosmopolitanism.

around pudong

The crazy-quilt skyline of Pudong is eye-popping—even more so when you realize that it's all been built since 1990. The government has moulded the area into the future of Shanghai, hoping to lure companies and thereby transform the municipality into Asia's business centre. In the 1930s, Pudong consisted of some warehouses, homes of a few merchants and mostly farmland. The only way to get to the east shore of the Huangpu was by ferry; now, there are also cable bridges and tunnels, including the Bund Sightseeing Tunnel, a Disney-esque kaleidoscope experience.

To entice foreign investors, Pudong is carved into zones with different business emphases, including a tax-free trade zone with bonded factories, a high-tech zone focused on biotech and microelectronics that aspires to be China's Silicon Valley, and an export-processing zone.

Along the riverbanks, the future in Pudong faces off the past on the Bund. The skyscraper colony across from the Bund is Lujiazui, a designated 'Wall Street' that includes the Shanghai Stock Exchange, the Diamond Exchange and dozens of multinational banks and investment houses. The stunning Jin Mao Tower, loosely shaped like a Chinese pagoda with Art Deco trimmings, looks a bit Gotham City on cloudy nights. The high-tech Grand Hyatt Shanghai on floors 53–87 is the world's highest hotel. Under construction next door is the Shanghai World Financial Centre, which was originally scheduled to be the tallest building on earth, until the 1997 Asian financial crisis interrupted the project for several years.

Shanghai's official nickname is the 'Pearl of the Orient', and thus the wacky Oriental Pearl TV Tower's pink and silver 'pearls' are a real tribute to the city. The 468-m (1,535-ft) tall love-it-or-hate-it icon, which has been likened to a spaceship and a hypodermic needle, transmits television and radio signals. From the Pearl pinnacle, the eight-lane-wide Century Avenue—which was modelled on Paris' Champs Elysées by the French architect of the Shanghai Grand Theatre—unfurls to Century Park, the

THIS PAGE: Pudong's other-worldly skyline includes the Oriental Pearl TV Tower and the dazzling Jin Mao Tower.
OPPOSITE: The psychedelic Bund Sightseeing Tunnel that takes visitors straight to Pudong.

city's largest, which also incorporates a wildlife park and picnic area, a miniature golf course and waterways complete with pedalboats.

As more and more multinationals have moved into Pudong, so have their foreign executives. And Pudong's wide-open space (at least compared to Puxi) has made it an expatriate family paradise. Compounds of three-storey, stand-alone houses with bikes on the front lawns and Buicks and Mercedes in the driveways look as if they are straight out of suburban California.

Other complexes offer ersatz Hawaiian sand beaches or European gentry gardens with canals and swans, and on the drawing board are more mini-towns with German and Victorian architectural themes. Executives' families sponsored by big names such as GM, Intel, Siemens, Nike and IBM also have several international schools, tennis courts, golf courses, Wal-Mart and other amenities at their disposal.

The government has consciously planned recreational, civic and cultural facilities to accompany the business monuments it has built in Pudong. There's the Shanghai Municipal Historical Museum (whose dioramas of old commercial streets don't look that different from Nanshi) and an impressive aquarium, with a huge underwater tunnel of sharks and fish. The Shanghai Science and Technology Museum, which shows IMAX movies, had exhibits overhauled and added by Canadian designers in 2005. The state-of-the-art Oriental Arts Centre, created by Frenchman Paul Andreu, has three theatres of different sizes. (Andreu also designed Pudong's soaring-seagull-like airport, which demoted Hongqiao to a domestic airport in 1999.)

But the Oriental Arts Centre doesn't get the kind of tour-de-force performances that the Shanghai Grand Theatre regularly books; in terms of bountiful and top-flight culture, art events, dining, effective public transportation and other lifestyle and intangible qualities, Pudong has a way to go. For now, many Shanghainese and foreigners stick to the adage, 'rather a bed in Puxi than an apartment in Pudong'.

...the 'Pearl of the Orient'.

Grand Hyatt Shanghai

Famous in Shanghai, as it soars above the city's skyline, the 420-m (1,375-ft) Jin Mao Tower lies east of the Huangpu River in Lujiazui, Pudong's fastest growing business and financial area. Occupying the 53rd to the 87th floor, Grand Hyatt Shanghai has become one of the most significant landmarks in the city. Given the accolade of the highest hotel in the world in 2000, by the *Guinness Book of Records*, it provides a giddying panorama of the city.

As you enter the reception area on the 54th floor, double height glass windows ensure full use of the incredible view. Beautiful columns of French limestone echo the architecture of the Bund, which seems minute, hundreds of metres below. The hotel is dominated by a breathtaking, 33-storey atrium that provides as dizzying a spectacle as the views outside.

Six high-speed glass elevators take you to the lavish guestrooms that capture the true

THIS PAGE: The dramatic yet chic sky pool with its marble finishing affords stunning views of the city.

OPPOSITE: Double height glass windows of the reception area make full use of the incredible view.

Beautiful columns of French limestone echo the architecture of the Bund.

essence of modern Chinese chic. Tang Dynasty calligraphy, engraved onto lacquer screens and Ming-style wedding cabinets, are a sharp contrast to the sleek modern lines of the interior architecture. Spacious bathrooms are adorned in glass and marble and have unsurpassed views of the city, for guests to admire while enjoying the ultimate power shower.

With 12 restaurants and bars scattered over the upper floors of the Jin Mao Tower there seems little reason to go down to ground level. Incorporating all possible tastes you can choose from French Brasserie style to up-market Italian, sleek Japanese to traditional Chinese with private balconies looking across Shanghai from the 54th floor.

For exclusive dining, Club Jin Mao offers the ultimate sophisticated setting, serving exquisite local Shanghainese cuisine. Canton, the hotel's speciality restaurant, provides a more intimate environment with authentic Cantonese dishes such as shark's fin, abalone and bird's nest soup. The Grand Café, open 24-hours, fuses Asian and Western cuisine in a modern and dramatic open space. The focal point for The Grill is the huge grill and rotisserie where you can watch your meat and seafood sizzle in front of you. At Kobachi you can enjoy the fun and relaxed atmosphere perched on a striking, central

bar enjoying the restaurant's specialities of sushi and yakitori. The Grand Hyatt Shanghai even has its own fast food restaurant, Food Live, where you can grab a casual meal on the run. All the restaurants make full use of their height and are dominated by the dramatic views of the city.

For Shanghai's most memorable cocktail visit Cloud 9. On the 87th floor it's the highest bar in the world, and, according to *Newsweek*, one of the world's greatest gathering places. The 360° views are staggering both in the daytime, when you look down onto the meandering river, the Bund, The Pearl Tower and Shanghai's

skyline beneath you, and at night-time when a dazzling show of neon lights spreads across the city. The stylized architecture has an ultra-modern finish in polished chrome and dark wood, and with an astounding capability to swing up to 75 cm (30 in) in the wind, you'll never be quite sure if you've had one drink too many.

The Grand Hyatt Shanghai also boasts the highest fitness centre in the world. A perfect place to build up your resistance to altitude it is also a heavenly retreat for both the mind and the body with a spacious and luxurious spa area. With a steam room, sauna and numerous spa pools, it provides

THIS PAGE (FROM TOP): Dine at Cucina and enjoy the view; Tang Dynasty calligraphy in the Grand Room; the 33-storey atrium dominates the hotel's interior.

OPPOSITE (FROM TOP): Colour tones warm the hotel lobby; the building towers above the Pudong skyline.

A short taxi-ride from the dizzying heights of your hotel room will take you across the Huangpu River to the historic Bund. Prestigious boutique malls containing luxury brands such as Armani, Cartier and Zegna and some of the city's finest dining experiences reside in the colonial style waterfront buildings. On the near side of the river is the famous landmark of the Oriental Pearl Tower the aquarium and the Tourist Tunnel make for remarkable, if somewhat quirky, attractions.

every indulgence in a state-of-the-art environment. The sky pool, with a somewhat dramatic infinity edge, allows you to exercise whilst taking in the breathtaking panorama of the Shanghai skyline.

For savvy business travellers the Business Centre provides every facility you should need including secretarial support, translation services and office equipment rental. There's a conference room along with numerous private rooms that can be rented for meetings 24 hours a day.

FACTS		
ROOMS	555
FOOD	Grand Cafe • Canton • Cucina • Kobachi • The Grill • Club Jin Mao
DRINK	Cloud 9 • Piano Bar • PU-Js • Patio • Wine Bar
FEATURES	business centre • fitness centre • indoor pool • spa
NEARBY	Lujiazui Finance and Trade District in Pudong
CONTACT	Jin Mao Tower, 88 Century Boulevard, Pudong, Shanghai, 200121 • telephone: +86.21.5049 1234 • facsimile: +86.21.5049 1111 • email: info@hyattshanghai.com • website: www.shanghai.grand.hyatt.com

PHOTOGRAPHS COURTESY OF GRAND HYATT SHANGHAI.

Pudong Shangri-La

With its magnificent new tower, Pudong Shangri-La, Shanghai is in a class of its own, with some of the city's most spacious rooms, dazzling new restaurants and bars, and the largest ballroom. The luxurious CHI spa, with its Himalayan-inspired décor and superb treatments, was also built along with a second, glassed-in, outdoor pool.

Spread over two towers, the hotel promises a sense of extreme spaciousness, spectacular views, ultra-modern facilities and a range of cuisines in trend-setting restaurants for its guests to enjoy. In the Lujiazui Finance and Trade Zone of Shanghai, the hotel is located on the east side of the Huangpu and offers outstanding views across the river to the legendary waterfront strip of the Bund, making it the ideal base whether you're travelling for business or pleasure.

The welcoming lobby evokes a sense of grandeur that continues right through the hotel. The huge expanse of highly polished marble is softened by elegant furniture and numerous Chinese panels. The light and airy rooms are some of the most spacious you'll find and are tastefully finished with elegant Chinese artefacts. Enormous windows throughout offer fantastic panoramic views.

The light and airy rooms are some of the most spacious you'll find...

With first-class facilities including the spa, two swimming pools, an outdoor tennis court, a fitness centre, steam bath, jacuzzi and a huge diversity of restaurants, Pudong Shangri-La caters for any indulgence for both staying guests and visitors.

Newly opened in 2005, Jade on 36 Restaurant and Bar, located in the hotel's new glass tower, promises an extraordinary dining experience. It begins with the walk-through the 4-m (14-ft)-tall rice bowl sculpture and continues with stunning views of the gleaming skyscrapers and meandering river below. The sophisticated, avant-garde

European cuisine from celebrated chef Paul Pairet completes the experience.

An abundance of Asian options include Yi Café, which incorporates eight show kitchens into one restaurant and offers flavours from China, Japan and India as well as Morocco and the Mediterranean. For Japanese cuisine, Nadaman Restaurant will provide an unforgettable evening—it also has three private dining rooms for that special occasion. Alternatively, try the Sushi Bar by Nadaman; one of the best in the city. A Chinese restaurant serves dishes from various regions of China. For Cantonese influences Fook Lam Moon specializes in shark's fin, bird's nest and abalone whilst offering inspiring views of the Bund through their floor-to-ceiling windows.

With a brand new Rolls Royce Phantom waiting to pick you up from the airport and smart, friendly staff welcoming you into the hotel, you may imagine you had just discovered Shangri-La itself.

THIS PAGE (FROM TOP): A Premier room facing the Bund affords fabulous views of Shanghai's skyline; dining at Nadaman offers pure sophistication.

OPPOSITE (FROM TOP): Pudong Shangri-La Shanghai sits proudly on the Huangpu; across the river, the Bund displays its charm.

FACTS		
ROOMS	981	
FOOD	Jade on 36 Restaurant and Bar • Nadaman • Yi Café • Sushi Bar by Nadaman • Gourmet • Fook Lam Moon • Chinese Restaurant •	
DRINK	The Bar • BATS • The Lounge • Lobby Lounge	
FEATURES	2 pools • tennis court • gym • spa • chauffer-driven limousine • business centre	
NEARBY	the Bund • Huangpu River	
CONTACT	33 Fu Cheng Road, Pudong, Shanghai, 200120 • telephone: +86.21.6882 8888 • facsimile: +86.21.6882 6688 • email: slpu@shangri-la.com • website: www.shangri-la.com	

East China Sea

Jiangsu

Changjiang (Yangzi River)

day-trips

Chongming Island

Changxing Island

Heng-sha Island

• Jiading

Suzhou

• **SHANGHAI**

Zhouzhuang ●

• Sheshan

• Songjiang

Zhejiang

• Jinshan

Hangzhou

Hangzhou Bay

suzhou

Marco Polo called it the 'Venice of the East'. Gentle Suzhou has a pretty serenity that trickles through its narrow interlocking canals, under its arched stone bridges and into its meticulously laid-out gardens. One of the oldest towns in the Yangzi basin, Suzhou still has remnants of its ancient protective moat. It is known for its exquisite embroidery, lustrous pearls and luscious silk (visit the Suzhou Silk Museum, which has live silkworms on display). Another of Suzhou's claims to fame is its women, widely said to be the most beautiful in China.

Suzhou, about 80 km (50 miles) northwest of Shanghai, boomed as a shipping hub after the magnificent Grand Canal was completed around AD 610. The longest artificial waterway in the world, the 1,800-km (1,118-mile) canal connected the Yellow and the Yangzi rivers and was a vital mechanism for trade and transportation from Hangzhou to Beijing. Many sections of the Grand Canal have long since silted over and become unnavigable, but south of the Yangzi, the water continues to flow. An overnight boat meandering along the Grand Canal remains one way to travel from Suzhou to Hangzhou.

At Suzhou's heart is a concentration of China's most perfect, formerly private gardens, built by intellectuals, painters, traders, officials and other elites who sought out the city as a retreat. The gardens are in fact on UNESCO's World Heritage list of treasures. As a microcosm of the earth, a Chinese classical garden has specific essentials including water, rocks, trees and plants, and man-made structures. Nature is not meant to be wild and random but painstakingly shaped and placed, so that a window or entryway might perfectly frame a lotus pool that has a stone island and pavilion in its centre, a willow tree at its edge, and a rippling reflection of this all in its water.

A walk through a Chinese garden is a succession of scenery snapshots. Suzhou's crème de la crème comprise the Humble Administrator's Garden—whose size is not humble compared to other gardens; Lion Grove, named for its weathered, contorted rockeries that resemble lions; Surging Wave Pavilion, whose perimeter is partially open

PAGE 192: *The bamboo forests near West Lake in Hangzhou.*

OPPOSITE AND THIS PAGE: *Suzhou has picturesque canals, gardens and ponds of blooming lotus.*

and whose snapshot scenes are thus unusual in incorporating the scenery and geography outside; and the Garden for Lingering, with an impressive 6.5-m (21-ft) tall rock from Lake Tai. The city's best garden, however, is its smallest: the masterfully condensed and detailed Garden of the Master of the Nets, which contains a fully-furnished Ming cottage and presents traditional music and dance performances in the evening.

Just northwest of Suzhou is Tiger Hill, a small but historically significant hill. King Helu of the Wu Kingdom was buried here in 496 BCE. According to legend, after the funeral, a white tiger appeared and sat on the king's gravesite as if to guard it, and hence the hill got its name. On the summit is the leaning Tiger Hill Pagoda, a seven-storey brick structure completed in AD 960 that began leaning about 400 years ago.

zhouzhuang

Step 900 years back in time in Zhouzhuang, the most renowned water town near Shanghai. Most water villages have evaporated; with its canal layout and geography still true to original form, Zhouzhuang today is one of a tiny breed.

Zhouzhuang has humpback stone bridges, canals, cobblestone paths, and wooden houses with tiled roofs that draw painters and art students to set up easels. A steady stream of artists and tour buses disembarking, added to the flood of eateries, souvenir and trinket stands, artisan workshops, freshwater pearl stores and galleries ready to greet them, has made Zhouzhuang a Disneyfied Chinese village/living-history museum, where the show has replaced most of the real.

The old town—south of the modern, concrete Zhouzhuang—has an entrance marked by the tall Quanfu Pagoda and the Ancient Memorial Archway (both of which are circa 1980s). Inside, all of the alleys are pedestrianized and the majority of the houses along the canals date from the Yuan, Ming or Qing dynasties.

The Zhang Residence, completed in 1449, is the oldest home open to the public. Alongside its main hall is a pond where boats could drop off visitors and then turn around. This abode of a former local official has six courtyards and 70 rooms.

South of the Zhangs' place is the Qing-era Chen Residence, which is even more impressive. A string of two-storey wooden halls, separated by courtyards, straddles both sides of the lane. The buildings are connected by a walkway on the top floor, an ancient Chinese version of a sky-bridge. The 100 rooms, with elaborate Qing furnishings and décor, include a large reception chamber, separate halls for men and women, and workshops for the craftspeople hired by the Chens.

A boat or gondola ride is a terrific way to explore Zhouzhuang's canal system, which was once devoted to moving rice, silk and pottery to Shanghai and points beyond via the Grand Canal. (The Zhouzhuang Museum has exhibits of locally-made Ming and Qing pottery and other crafts.) If you stop for a meal, try the local speciality, wansanti, a pork knuckle simmered in a sweet-salty soup. For a glimpse of everyday life with ordinary villagers and fishermen and today's smaller homes, walk along Quanfu Bridge. Zhouzhuang, less than 40 km (25 miles) from Suzhou, can be visited on its own or combined with a trip to Suzhou.

hangzhou

The capital of the Southern Song Dynasty and the southern terminus of the Grand Canal, Hangzhou in the 13th century was the place to be in China. In 1275, its population was 1.75 million. It was 'the finest, most splendid city in the world', declared Marco Polo, 'where so many pleasures may be found that one fancies oneself to be in Paradise.' Currently, the capital of Zhejiang Province may not live up to Polo's pronouncement (history saw it ransacked and devastated several times, from the 1861, during the Taiping Rebellion, to the Cultural

Revolution), but Hangzhou has retained much of its paradise-like beauty. It also has the trappings of a sophisticated Chinese city, with Giorgio Armani and Dolce & Gabbana shops and Xihu Tiandi, a sister of Shanghai's Xintiandi, at its famous West Lake.

It is West Lake that has been the centuries-old font of Hangzhou's beauty. Decorated with gardens, temples and pavilions, the 14-km- (8-mile-) circumference freshwater lake was a favourite of Chinese emperors, poets and scholars, who memorialized it in their writing and work. As a result, West Lake has amassed a portfolio of historical and literary spots. When the lake is partly bathed in mist, it's breathtaking.

The lake is divided by two causeways, and getting around on foot or by bike is easy. You can also hop on ferries that cruise to several stops around the lake, or rent a paddle boat (and a strong boatman to power it, or DIY).

Some of West Lake's top features: Solitary Hill Island, lying in the lake's northern part, has the Zhejiang Provincial Museum; Xiaoying Island is dotted with lotus ponds and has a nine-turn bridge and an excellent view of three stone pagodas on the lake; Red Carp Pond is thick with them.

To the west of West Lake is the Temple of the Soul's Retreat (Lingyin Temple), which at one time housed 3,000 monks. As you trek up to the temple, notice the Buddhist images on the limestone cliffside—there are supposedly 470, which were made between the 10th and 14th centuries. The best-loved is the semi-reclining, laughing Buddha, whose wide grin was carved in AD 1000. On the temple grounds is an inscription of a couplet written by Qing emperor Kangxi and a 20-m (65-ft)-high camphor wood statue of Sakyamuni Buddha.

Hangzhou is famed for its tea; the best-known variety is called Longjing (Dragon Well), and is named after a spring located just outside the city. The hillsides surrounding Hangzhou are carved with tea-crop terraces. You might catch women plucking tender, bright green leaves from the bushes, depending on the season. Downhill in Dragon Well Village's small shops, men roast the leaves by tossing them in hot woks, letting off a heady fragrance.

THIS PAGE: Fuchun Resort's interior design details.
OPPOSITE: A rare and picturesque snowfall at Fuchun.

When the lake is partly bathed in mist, it's breathtaking.

Fuchun Resort

Almost seven centuries ago, Huang Gongwang, a master of the Yuan Dynasty, retired to his hometown of Fuyang in the Fuchun Mountains and immersed himself in a life of cultural leisure and a passion for painting. He devoted 10 years to creating a scroll titled 'Dwelling in the Fuchun Mountains'. Now considered a national treasure, the scroll describes a vision of harmony where man and nature are one. Using Gongwang's writings as inspiration, Fuchun Resort has created a tranquil retreat where natural harmony and peace bring respite from the hectic pace of Shanghai.

Just over 100 km (62 miles) from Shanghai, Fuchun Resort is set amongst the serenity of rural China and tranquillity and relaxation permeate the stunning resort. Immersed in the traditional countryside, surrounded by beautiful mountain ranges and tea plantations, guests can lead a holistic lifestyle taking in the fresh air and absorbing the breathtaking natural beauty.

The resort is built in traditional Fuyangese style on the edge of a large lake. During the day, cool mists create an alluring and peaceful beauty while at night the resort's lights reflect in the water. The style,

THIS PAGE (FROM TOP): Every part of this resort displays contemporary Chinese style, the boutique is just one example; Fuchun is set on a serene lake creating a superb ambience.

OPPOSITE (FROM TOP): The Lake Lounge is one place to take in the stunning environment; all rooms and suites come with vast windows bringing the beauty inside.

Whatever you have come here for, your romantic visions will be met.

surrounded by dark pillars is a sanctuary in itself with tall glass doors leading outside to the veranda with jacuzzi.

The indulgences continue with exceptional dining opportunities including Asian Corner; authentic with its use of dark woods, red lanterns and rosewood panels. Club 8, a rural counterpart to the famous T8 restaurant in Xintiandi, provides sophisticated fusion cuisine. The more relaxed Lake and Aqua Lounges offer sweeping views across the Fuchun Resort whilst you sit back and enjoy their snacks, cocktails and healthy juices. Whatever you have come here for, your romantic visions will be met. This is the China you imagine.

though deeply rooted in Chinese tradition, is spacious and modern. The rooms are beautiful in their simplicity, and floor-to-ceiling windows dominate the space.

Fuchun Resort has unprecedented facilities and include China's finest international standard and award-winning 18-hole golf course set amongst a working tea plantation. There are also tennis courts and a spa with treatments enticingly named Summer Breeze and Silk Cocoon. After a massage, some tai chi and yoga, the city's stresses will have completely left your body. A magnificent, blackstone indoor pool

FACTS

ROOMS	70 • 13 villas
FOOD	Club 8 • Asian Corner
DRINK	Lake Lounge • Aqua Lounge
FEATURES	spa • indoor pool • tennis • golf • driving range • lake • yoga • tai chi
NEARBY	Hangzhou
CONTACT	Fuyang Section, Hangfu Yanjiang Road, Hangzhou, Zhejiang, 311401 • telephone: +86.571.6346 1111 • facsimile: +86.571.6346 1222 • email: reservation@fuchunresort.com • website: www.fuchunresort.com

PHOTOGRAPHS COURTESY OF FUCHUN RESORT.

Sheraton Suzhou Hotel + Towers

THIS PAGE: The Chinese-style architecture and pagodas that decorate the hotel make this a special location to enjoy your truly Chinese experience.

OPPOSITE (CLOCKWISE FROM LEFT): The extensive grounds provide all facilities; canals surround the hotel; The landscaped gardens offer peaceful sanctuary.

After sight-seeing and partying hard in the 'Paris of the East', visit the more relaxed and romantic setting of Suzhou the 'Venice of the East', dubbed so by Marco Polo when he visited in the 13th century. Only one hour from Shanghai by train or car, Suzhou is a thriving commercial city in its own right and has a stunning historical heritage.

Located on Lake Tai, one of China's five biggest freshwater lakes measuring 68 km (42 miles) long, and criss-crossed by canals fed from the delta of the Yangzi River, Suzhou is a stunning city. Steeped in history it is filled with ancient bridges, temples and pagodas and surrounded by the old city wall. Boat tours are the best way to experience the feel and architecture of Suzhou and take you through the narrow, weeping willow lined canals to visit the remaining original gates to the city, temples and other local sites of interest.

The Sheraton Suzhou Hotel and Towers lies within the city centre and is a luxury base from which to explore. The hotel's Chinese-style architecture, pagodas, canals, beautifully landscaped gardens and lily ponds reflect the city itself and provide a serene and calming atmosphere.

The comfortably furnished rooms are light and spacious and include all modern facilities. Seventy exclusive tower rooms have been tailor-made essentially for business travellers with Internet and fax facilities and their own private check in and butler service.

Within the hotel you can relax by the picturesque outdoor pool, enjoy a refreshing afternoon tea or early evening cocktail from the Garden Lounge whilst overlooking the beautiful canals below. Or, for those inclined, enlist in a game of tennis whilst

...pagodas, canals, beautifully landscaped gardens and lily ponds reflect the city itself...

surrounded by the hotel's peaceful gardens. After a day of wandering the narrow streets of Suzhou, you can return for a relaxing massage or re-invigorating workout in the fitness centre where a second indoor Roman-style pool caters for the colder months.

Overlooking the hotel gardens, Garden Brasserie is set within a dramatic atrium with an elegant mezzanine level. The towering columns and sophisticated black furnishings completes the stylish setting. With both inside and al fresco seating you can enjoy a variety of both Western and Asian dishes.

There is also Riva's for a more relaxed atmosphere with its wood fire pizza oven and late night entertainment. But, wherever you spend your evenings at the Sheraton Suzhou, it's sure to be a memorable one.

FACTS		
	ROOMS	400
	FOOD	The Garden Brasserie • Celestial Court • Riva's • Delicatessen and Bakery
	DRINK	Garden Lounge • Pagoda Lounge
	FEATURES	health and fitness centre • 2 pools • tennis court • business centre • limousine service
	NEARBY	Suzhou • Shanghai • Wuxi
	CONTACT	259 Xin Shi Road, Suzhou, Jiangsu, 215007 • telephone: +86.512.6510 3388 • facsimile: +86.512.6510 0888 • email: sheraton.suzhou@sheraton.com • website: www.sheraton.com/suzhou

PHOTOGRAPHS COURTESY OF SHERATON SUZHOU HOTEL + TOWERS.

index

index

picturecredits + acknowledgements

The publisher would like to thank the following for permission to reproduce their photographs:

239 Restaurant + Bar 37
Andrea Pistolesi/Tips 72
Banyan Tree Spa Shangai back cover (spa)
Bund 18 60 (left), 61 (below), 165 (left)
China Newsphoto/alt.TYPE Images 59
Claro Cortes/alt.TYPE Images 176
David Hartung/OnAsia 15, 17 (top), 178 (below)
Don Klumpp/Tips 73 (below)
Digital Vision/Getty Images 64
Edmund Ho/Jambu Studio back cover (street, dumplings), 5, 14 (left), 19 (below), 39 (top), 44, 66 (below), 163 (below), 165 (right), 177 (below)
Face back cover (sculpture), 67 (top), 69 (below)
Firefly Productions/Corbis 45 (below)
Four Seasons Hotel Shanghai 33
Fritz Hoffman/documentChina 54 (top), 55 (left), 57 (below), 172 (below), 173, 174, 175, 180
Fuchun Resort back cover (floral detail), front cover (cutlery), 197 (below), 198, 199
Gerhard Jörën/OnAsia 20 (right)

Grand Hyatt Shanghai 2, 167 (below)
Greg Girard/documentChina 29, 47, 56, 62 (top)
Jörg Sundermann front cover (bird, fish and door handle)
Juan Manuel Silva/Tips 55 (right)
JW Marriott front flap (below)
Kathleen's 5 Restaurant + Bar 41, 63
Kelly-Mooney Photography/Corbis 6
Keren Su/Corbis 204–205
Liu Liqun/Corbis 192
Luca Invernizzi Tettoni 193
Morgan Ommer 22 (below), 26, 33 (top), 38, 53 (below), 58, 70
Natalie Behring/OnAsia front cover (face), 25, 167 (top)
Number D Gallery 74 (below)
Paul Harris/OnAsia 22
Peter Charlesworth/OnAsia back cover (boat), 194
Philippe Dureuil front cover (alley), back cover (villa), 16 (right), 17 (top), 20 (left), 23, 24 (below), 30 (below), 34 (top), 40 (top), 46, 50 (top), 54 (below), 66 (top), 68, 69 (top), 71 (top), 73 (top), 158, 161, 162, 164, 166, 168, 181, 185
Photodisc/Inmagine 4–5, 196 (below)
Reuters/alt.TYPE Images 43 (top & below), 57 (top), 171 (top)
Scott A. Woodward photography 171 (below)

Shanghai Municipal Tourism Administrative Commission 196 (top)
Shanghai Tang back flap (top)
Shanghart Gallery 48
Simply Life 197 (top)
Sin Kam Cheong 21, 28, 39 (below), 42, 45 (top), 62 (centre), 64 (left), 160, 163 (top), 177 (top), 184
Stefan Irvine/OnAsia 24 (top)
Steven Harris/OnAsia 31
Thai Gallery 50
The Creek Art Centre 52, 74 (top), 75, 178 (top)
The Image Bank/Getty Images 8–9
Three on the Bund front flap (top), 32, 34 (top), 35, 36, 53
Vincent Long/OnAsia 61 (top)
Xintiandi front cover (cushions), 16, 51, 172 (top)
Yang Liu/Corbis 170
Yè Shanghai front flap (centre), back cover (bicycle), 40 (below)
Zoë Jaques 15 (top), 17 (below), 18, 30 (top), 49, 62 (below), 67 (below), 169, 182

The publishers would like to thank Michelle D. Wan, Angelo Sabatelli, Thierry Alix, Jereme Leung, Tan Su Lyn, Emma Davies, David Schlosser, Ping Ping, Tina Kanagaratnam, Dimitri Kaczmarek, Celina Chew and Audrey Koh for their help and support.

directory

hotels/serviced apartments

88 Xintiandi (page 76)
380 Huang Pi Nan Road
Shanghai, 200021
telephone : +86.21.5383 8833
facsimile : +86.21.5383 8877
inquiry@88xintiandi.com
www.88xintiandi.com

Four Seasons Hotel Shanghai (page 78)
500 Weihai Road
Shanghai, 200041
telephone : +86.21.6256 8888
facsimile : +86.21.6256 5678
www.fourseasons.com/shanghai

Fuchun Resort (page 200)
Fuyang Section, Hangfu Yanjiang Road
Hangzhou, Zhejiang, 311401
telephone : +86.571.6346 1111
facsimile : +86.571.6346 1222
reservation@fuchunresort.com
www.fuchunresort.com

Grand Hyatt Shanghai (page 186)
Jin Mao Tower, 88 Century Boulevard
Pudong, Shanghai, 200121
telephone : +86.21.5049 1234
facsimile : +86.21.5049 1111
info@shanghai.grand.hyatt.com
www.shanghai.grand.hyatt.com

JW Marriott Hotel Shanghai (page 80)
Tomorrow Square, 399 Nanjing West Road
Shanghai, 200003
telephone : +86.21.5359 4969
facsimile : +86.21.6375 5988
mhrs.shajw.reservations@marriotthotels.com
www.marriotthotels.com/shajw

Pudong Shangri-La (page 190)
33 Fu Cheng Road, Pudong
Shanghai, 200120
telephone : +86.21.6882 8888
facsimile : +86.21.6882 6688
slpu@shangri-la.com
www.shangri-la.com

Shama Luxe at Xintiandi (page 82)
Block 18 Lakeville Regency, Lane 168
Shun Chang Road, Luwan District
Shanghai, 200021
telephone : +86.21.6385 1818
info.shanghai@shama.com
www.shama.com

Sheraton Suzhou Hotel + Towers (page 202)
259 Xin Shi Road
Suzhou, Jiangsu, 215007
telephone : +86.512.6510 3388
facsimile : +86.512.6510 0888
sheraton.suzhou@sheraton.com
www.sheraton.com/suzhou

The Westin Shanghai (page 84)
Bund Centre, 88 Henan Central Road
Shanghai, 200002
telephone : +86.21.6335 8888
facsimile : +86.21.6335 2888
rsvns-shanghai@westin.com
www.westin.com/shanghai

restaurants

239 Restaurant + Bar (page 86)
239 Shimen Yi Road
Shanghai, 200041
telephone : +86.21.6253 2837
facsimile : +86.21.6253 2837
marketing@239shanghai.com
www.239shanghai.com

Azul + Viva (page 88)
18 Dong Ping Road
Shanghai, 200031
telephone : +86.21.6433 1172
facsimile : +86.21.6433 1173
marketing@azulviva.com
www.azulviva.com

Bali Laguna (page 90)
Jing'An Park, 189 Huashan Road
Shanghai, 200040
telephone : +86.21.6248 6970
facsimile : +86.21.6248 6961
fromedwin@gmail.com
www.bali-laguna.com

Bar Rouge (page 92)
7th Floor, Bund 18
18 Zhongshan East Road
Shanghai, 200002
telephone : +86.21.6339 1199
facsimile : +86.21.6339 2979
barrouge@volmail.cc
www.resto18.com

Barbarossa (page 94)
231 Nanjing Road West, People's Park
Shanghai, 200003
telephone : +86.21.6318 0220
facsimile : +86.21.6318 0219
jennifer.green@barbarossa.com.cn
www.barbarossa.com.cn

Face (page 96)
118 Ruijin 2 Road, #4 Building
Ruijin Guest House
Shanghai, 200020
telephone : +86.21.6466 4328
facsimile : +86.21.6415 8913

Kathleen's 5 Restaurant + Bar (page 98)
5th Floor, Shanghai Art Museum
325 Nanjing West Road
Shanghai, 200003
telephone : +86.21.6327 2221
facsimile : +86.21.6327 0004
info@kathleens5.com
www.kathleens5.com

Lan Kwai Fong, Park 97 (page 100)
2A Gaolan Road, Fuxing Park
Shanghai, 200020
telephone : +86.21.5383 2328
facsimile : +86.21.6387 4716
park97@lkfgroup.com
www.lankwaifong.com

Mesa Manifesto (page 102)
748 Julu Road
Shanghai, 200040
telephone : +86.21.6289 9108
facsimile : +86.21.6289 9138
info@mesa-manifesto.com
www.mesa-manifesto.com

Sasha's (page 104)
11 Dongping Road
Shanghai, 200021
telephone : +86.21.6474 6166
facsimile : +86.21.6474 6170
reservations@sashas-shanghai.com
www.sashas-shanghai.com

Sens + Bund (page 106)
6th Floor, Bund 18
18 Zhongshan East Road
Shanghai, 200002
telephone : +86.21.6323 9898
facsimile : +86.21.6323 8797
sensandbund@volmail.cc
www.resto18.com

Simply Thai (page 108)
Corner of Ma Dang and Xing Ye Road
Shanghai, 200021
telephone : +86.21.6326 2088
facsimile : +86.21.6384 6522
5C Dong Ping Road, Shanghai, 200031
telephone : +86.21.6445 9551
Lane 3338, 28–29 Hongmei Road
Shanghai, 201103
telephone : +86.21.6465 8955
enquiry@simplythai-sh.com
www.simplythai-sh.com

T8 Restaurant (page 110)
8 Xintiandi North, Lane 181 Taicang Road
Shanghai, 200021
telephone : +86.21.6355 8999
facsimile : +86.21.6311 4999
t8@ghmhotels.com
www.ghmhotels.com

Tan Wai Lou (page 112)
5th Floor, Bund 18
18 Zhongshan Dong Road
Shanghai, 200002
telephone : +86.21.6339 1188
facsimile : +86.21.6323 8789
tanwailou@volmail.cc
www.resto18.com

Thai Gallery (page 114)
127 Datian Road by Beijing West Road
Shanghai, 200041
telephone : +86.21.6217 9797
facsimile : +86.21.6271 5983
fromedwin@gmail.com
www.thaigallery.com.cn

Va Bene (page 116)
Lane 181 Taicang Road, Xintiandi
Shanghai, 200021
telephone : +86.21.6311 2211
facsimile : +86.21.5306 6138
vabene@vabeneshanghai.com
www.vabeneshanghai.com

Yè Shanghai (page 118)
388 Huang Pi Nan Road, Xintiandi
Shanghai, 200021
telephone : +86.21.6311 2323
facsimile : +86.21.6311 3311
yss@elite-concepts.com
www.elite-concepts.com

ZIN wine bar + grill (page 120)
No. 2 Lane 66, Dan Shui Road
Shanghai, 200020
telephone : +86.21.6385 8123
facsimile : +86.21.6385 1312
zin@elite-concepts.net
www.elite-concepts.net

shops

Annabel Lee Shanghai (page 122)
Bund flagship store: No. 1, No. 8 Lane
Zhongshan Dong Yi Road, the Bund
Shanghai, 200002
telephone : +86.21.6445 8218
facsimile : +86.21.6323 0093
Xintiandi store: Unit 3, House 3, North Block
Xintiandi, Lane 181 Taicang Road, Xintiandi
Shanghai, 200021
telephone : +86.21.6320 0045
facsimile : +86.21.6320 0045
info@annabel-lee.com
www.annabel-lee.com

Annly's Antique (page 124)
No. 68, Lane 7611 Zhongchun Road
Shanghai, 201101
telephone : +86.21.6406 0242
facsimile : +86.21.6405 7322
anntique@online.sh.cn
www.annlychyn.com

Bund 18 (page 126)
18 Zhongshan East Road
Shanghai, 200002
telephone : +86.21.6323 7066
facsimile : +86.21.6323 7060
info@bund18.com
www.bund18.com

Hong Merchant (page 128)
No. 3 Lane 372 Xing Guo Road
Shanghai, 200052
telephone : +86.21.6283 2696
facsimile : +86.21.6283 9721
jpweber@uninet.cn, an-cecil@online.sh.cn
www.hongmerchant.com

Hu + Hu (page 130)
Cao Bao Road, Alley 1885, #8
Shanghai, 201101
telephone : +86.21.3431 1212
facsimile : +86.21.5486 2160
hu-hu@online.sh.com
www.hu-hu.com

Jooi Design (page 132)
2nd Floor International Artist Factory
Taikang Road Lane 210
Shanghai, 200025
telephone : +86.21.6473 6193
facsimile : +86.21.6415 2386
studio@jooi.com
www.jooi.com

Number D Gallery (page 134)
2nd Floor, Building 15, 1518 Xikang Road
Shanghai, 200060
telephone : +86.21.6226 2109
facsimile : +86.21.6299 4289
info@numberD.com
www.numberD.com

Shanghai Tang (page 136)
Jinjiang Hotel, Shop E
59 Maoming South Road
Shanghai, 200020
telephone : +86.21.5466 3006
facsimile : +86.21.5466 3011
Shangri-La Hotel, Lobby Level,
33 Fu Cheng Road, Pudong
Shanghai, 200120
telephone : +86.21.5877 6632
facsimile : +86.21.5877 6635
Xintiandi Plaza, 15 Xintiandi North Block
181 Taicang Road
Shanghai, 200021
telephone : +86.21.6384 1601
facsimile : +86.21.6384 4106
contactus@shanghaitang.com
www.shanghaitang.com

Shanghai Trio (page 138)
Xintiandi Boutique
Lane 181 Taicang Road, Shanghai, 200021
telephone : +86.21.6355 2974
Showroom : House 6, Lane 37
Fuxing West Road, Shanghai, 200031
telephone : +86.21.6433 8901
facsimile : +86.21.6473 7819
shanghaitrio@shanghaitrio.com.cn
www.shanghaitrio.com

Shanghart Gallery (page 140)
50 Moganshan Road, Building 16 + 18
Shanghai, 200060
telephone : +86.21.6359 3923
facsimile : +86.21.6359 4570
info@shanghartgallery.com
www.shanghartgallery.com

Simply Life (page 142)
Corner of Ma Dang and Xing Ye Road
Shanghai, 200021
telephone : +86.21.6326 2088
facsimile : +86.21.6384 6522
9 Dong Ping Road
Shanghai, 200031
telephone : +86.21.3406 0509
facsimile : +86.21.3406 5509
enquiry@simplylife-sh.com
www.simplylife-sh.com

Three on the Bund (page 146)
5 Zhongshan Dong Yi Road
Shanghai, 200002
telephone : +86.21.6323 3355
facsimile : +86.21.6323 3344
info@on-the-bund.com
www.threeonthebund.com

Xintiandi (page 152)
North Block: Lane 181 Taicang Road
South Block: Lane 123 Xing Ye Road
Shanghai, 200021
telephone : +86.21.6311 2288
info@xintiandi.com
www.xintiandi.com

spas

Banyan Tree Spa Shanghai (page 154)
Level 3 The Westin Shanghai
Bund Centre, 88 Henan Central Road
Shanghai, 200002
telephone : +86.21.6335 1888
facsimile : +86.21.6335 1113
spa-shanghai@banyantree.com
www.banyantreespa.com/shanghai

Mandara Spa (page 156)
6th Floor, JW Marriott Hotel,
Tomorrow Square, 399 Nanjing West Road
Shanghai, 200003
telephone : +86.21.5359 4969
facsimile : +86.21.5852 1155
infochina@minornet.com
www.mspa-international.com